1989

WRITING
LITERARY FEATURES

COMMUNICATION TEXTBOOK SERIES
Jennings Bryant—Editor

Journalism
Maxwell McCombs—Advisor

BERNER • Writing Literary Features

FENSCH • The Sports Writing Handbook

TITCHENER • Reviewing the Arts

WRITING
LITERARY FEATURES

R. Thomas Berner
The Pennsylvania State University

LEA LAWRENCE ERLBAUM ASSOCIATES, PUBLISHERS
1988 Hillsdale, New Jersey   Hove and London

Parts of this book originally appeared as Journalism monograph Number 99, *Literary Newswriting: The Death of an Oxymoron*, and are reprinted by permission of the Association for Education in Journalism and Mass Communication.

The newspaper stories in this book are reprinted with permission and a copyright notice appears with each story.

With the exception of all remarks attributed to Richard Ben Cramer and some of the remarks attributed to Eric P. Best, the comments by the journalists whose stories are analyzed in this book were made in private correspondence with the author and remain the property of the originator. Cramer's remarks were made in a telephone interview, and some of Best's comments appeared in the December 1981 *Gannetteer*.

Lawrence Erlbaum Associates, Inc., Publishers
365 Broadway
Hillsdale, New Jersey   07642

Cover, production, and interior
design: Robin Marks Weisberg

Library of Congress Cataloging in Publication Data
Berner, R. Thomas.
    Writing literary features / by R. Thomas Berner.
      p.   cm.
    Bibliography: p.
    Includes index.
    ISBN 0-8058-0278-9. ISBN 0-8058-0279-7 (pbk.)
    1. Feature writing. 2. Style, Literary. 3. Journalism—
Authorship.   I. Title.
PN4784.F37B47 1988
070.4′4—dc 19

                            88-3846
                            CIP

Printed in the United States of America
10 9 8 7 6 5 4 3 2 1

This volume is dedicated to the late *Joseph Jay Rubin*, Professor Emeritus of American Literature, whose course on Masters of American Literature included journalists, which encouraged me.

Contents

Introduction

WHERE THIS BOOK FITS

"Every story doesn't lend itself to creative writing," Everett S. Allen (1979), the editorial page editor of the New Bedford, Massachusetts, *Standard-Times*, once wrote, "but there ought to be someone on every newpaper who recognizes such a story when it comes along and who can do something about it—who can create a piece that is an invitation to the reader not simply because of what it says, but also because of the manner in which it says it" (p. 5). Such a person would no doubt write the story using literary techniques. This book shows beginning journalists what many of those techniques are and how they are applied in newspaper writing.

Although I have titled this book *Writing Literary Features*, I would argue that modern journalists should not categorize stories as hard news or feature or literary feature, but should recognize that given the complex nature of life, the modern journalist needs a variety of writing approaches to satisfactorily explain the world to readers. Most of the stories in this book did not come from the feature pages of newspapers but from the news sections, yet they read like feature stories.

Writing should be viewed as what journalists do to shape the results of their reporting. If the facts best lend themselves to hard news (the inverted pyramid), that is the way the story should be written. But if the facts demand an essay or editorial or a literary feature, then that is the way the story should be written. *Content* and *function*—not the section the story will appear in the newspaper—should dictate form.

This book can be used in more than one course. For feature writing courses, *Writing Literary Features* can serve as the main text. One of this book's strengths is the attention it pays to how the reporters gathered the information that they eventually put into a literary shape. *Writing Literary Features* is equally useful in a newswriting or reporting course that explores various writing techniques. And anyone teaching public affairs or depth reporting would find this a useful supplementary text because some of the stories are in-depth public affairs reports. At Penn State, parts of the manuscript have been used in courses in feature writing, public affairs reporting, and editing.

Further, this book discusses the issues surrounding literary features—the issues of fact and form and factuality, and of truth and objectivity and reality. Philosophical and practical angles are explored. Whatever the course, however, this book assumes some knowledge and background in journalism. This is a book in basic literary feature writing, not basic journalism.

A CASE FOR GOOD WRITING

As any teacher of reporting knows, a well-written story is favored over a ho-hum story. And as editors, writing coaches, and pollsters have long said, newspapers need good writing. "Readers want to be informed. Yet we make it such a chore," George Rodgers (1983), an assistant managing editor at the *Baltimore Sun*, said. "Too many of our stories mash facts together with no more structure than a tottering inverted pyramid." Added Jon Franklin (1983), formerly of the *Sun*, a two-time winner of the Pulitzer prize for feature writing and the author of *Writing For Story*: "The public wants us to tell them a story, and is willing to pay handsomely for it." And William M. Chase (1982), an English professor at Stanford, wrote: "Journalists must put a certain degree of attractive enticement in their stories, if those stories are to be read by a passive audience that has learned to ask of newpapers that they provide more than stock-market figures, weather reports, or baseball scores" (p. 3). Literary features help accomplish that goal and make a newspaper more readable.

Recognizing that the reader must be served, the *Stockton* (California) *Record* published a five-part series on crime in which Eric P. Best and Patricia A. Donahue used literary techniques. "The fictionalized tone of the writing," Best said (1981), "with names changed but otherwise documented from interviews and the public record, was employed to promote greater reader interest and give the reporter more stylistic room in which to capture the sense of the story" (p. 16). A story from the Best–Donahue series appears in this book.

Another literary stylist is Mike Sager of *The Washington Post*, who writes with the competition in mind. "The video age," he noted, "is upon us" (personal communication, October, 1981). Sager made that statement to argue the point that newspaper stories had to be better written to compete for attention in a multimedia world that offers so much instant gratification merely by turning a knob. Sager said: "Give the readers vivid stories, stories that supply their own soundtrack and internal visuals." A Sager story appears in this book.

THE LITERARY FEATURE
AND JOURNALISM

Journalists use literary techniques to weave a story based on facts. They rely on scene-setting, relevant description, storytelling, logical development, plotting, and perspective. They maintain a literary thread throughout. A literary feature is more than one scene and a string of direct quotations; it is a consciously planned story designed with pattern and purpose in mind. Literary features have a beginning, middle, and end.

Some may argue that it is impossible to write in a literary style in newpapers, the implication being that anything literary is made up. But that attitude confuses content and technique. Newspaper stories are based on events and the journalists who write the stories attempt to portray the events factually. To use a phrase from *The Literature of Fact: Literary Nonfiction in American Writing* by Ronald Weber (1980), journalists are committed to ''the authority of fact'' (p. 49). The fiction writer can make up stories; the journalist, Weber said, ''is forced away from the [writing] desk and his own imagination and into an untidy world in which he must deal with events and people as they come to him'' (p. 51). The journalists represented in this book speak to those problems, and their stories show what journalists can do when the neat scene that would provide the perfect transition does not exist.

All information—factual or imaginary—must be shaped into a presentable form. Journalists attempt to reshape the facts as honestly as they can figure the facts occurred. Journalists use literary techniques as a way of giving shape to the facts of an untidy world. ''Today's well-written story,'' Franklin (1983) said, ''offers the reader a coherent view of a situation and shows him (as opposed to telling him) how the facts relate to the human condition'' (p. 17).

THE SELECTION PROCESS

I am interested in technique and content and not in any special order. I have challenged the journalists in this book whenever I thought their content seemed made up. I have asked for sources of some of the information in these stories, especially when information was attributed to a person's state of mind. When I have heard that the facts in a story were challenged, I have tried to determine the truth. When a particular writing approach was used, I challenged the writer's right to do that. I asked if an editor (or two) had been consulted; had the style been determined in advance or dictated by the substance of the story. In other words, I have examined each story in this book both for style and content because it is my conviction that if the facts cannot be verified, then the genre, no matter what the technique, cannot be journalism.

Books such as this one imply that only a limited number of ways exists to write a certain type of story, that there is only one way to write about the changing of the seasons or illegal alliens or coal miners fighting a bureaucracy. Novice writers wrongly infer that books such as this endorse an eternal formula. "I'm going to write a sidebar on a policeman's funeral," the novice says. "Let me check *Writing Literary Features* to see how it's done." No. Each story here is unique. Each was created out of a combination of facts of a particular situation and the talent of the particular writer. Another writer would have shaped the facts differently—and just as well. This book contains no formulas, save one: Good writing is hard work. There are no shortcuts.

ABOUT THIS BOOK

This book and a monograph I wrote titled *Literary Newswriting: The Death of an Oxymoron* (1986) grew from the same research. The monograph represents my scholarly analysis of the subject. This book represents the practical application of what I have learned.

ACKNOWLEDGMENTS

My appreciation to Sally Atwood, who helped gather material for this book; to Thomas F. Magner, Associate Dean for Research and Graduate Studies in the College of Liberal Arts at Penn State, who provided funding (and has, unrelated to this project, since retired); to Bruce M. Swain of the University of Georgia, who steered me in the right direction; to Maxwell McCombs, Warren Burkett, and Rebecca Schorin of the University of Texas at Austin, whose analysis helped me develop my ideas; to H. Eugene Goodwin, a colleague who read several versions in manuscript and who appears in chapter 10 as the former Washington reporter turned journalism professor and journalism ethicist (he is the author of *Groping for Ethics in Journalism*).

Chapter One
Literary Techniques

THE ANTECEDENTS
OF LITERARY NEWSWRITING

Today's literary newswriting in a newspapers has its roots in the new journalism movement of the late 1960s and early 1970s. But that does not mean that literary newswriting is something new. Literature and journalism have co-existed for at least 4 centuries, with one scholar suggesting that 16th century journalism took the form of the printed ballad. The scholar, Lennard J. Davis (1983), takes the position that the printed ballad of 4 centuries ago was likely to be read immediately after the event written about in the ballad. That type of ballad is unlike the ballad of a wandering minstrel, which recounted historical exploits and was useful even years after it was first composed.

Other scholars also record journalists using literary techniques more than 3 centuries ago. But during the period, literature and journalism split, and as a result scholars would not recognize the literary aspects of journalism until late in the 19th century. A good source of literarily styled newswriting from that century is *A Treasury of Great Reporting*, which republishes stories by journalists such as Daniel Defoe, Charles Dickens, Horace Greeley, James Gordon Bennett, Henry Villard, Mark Twain, Stephen Crane, Richard Harding Davis, Damon Runyon, John Gunther, Ernest Hemingway, William L. Shirer, Rebecca West, and accounts of a tea party in Boston, the fall of Mexico City, the charge of the Light Brigade, a labor rally in Britain, the degradation of Captain Dreyfus, the execution of Mata Hari, and the defeat of the Bonus Army.

Literary journalism has obviously been around for centuries. What we see today is perhaps only a polished and sophisticated version of what was done many times during the past 4 centuries. Today's literary newswriting reflects the process of evolution in all newswriting. As the late James E. Murphy (1974) explained: "What is now billed as a literary genre is the product of gradual development and a reflection of the times more than it is a radical innovation" (p. 34).

As with its antecedents, modern literary newswriting focuses on people rather than topics. Typically, such stories portray character. They are marked by forward movement, suspense, or dramatic tension and a climax.

Current literary feature writing in newspapers owes its existence to what scholars, writers, and critics consider new journalism circa 1970. In the new journalism, many scholars agree that style often was emphasized over substance. And although literary feature writing relies on style, the facts are not sacrificed for stylistic effect. Reporting is as much of the essence of a literary feature as is writing style. Documentation is essential. Jon Franklin (1987) stressed in an article in *Journalism Educator* that literary journalists "never take liberties with the facts . . . because to do so would be to pull punches and cheapen the story" (p. 13).

And what are the virtues of modern literary newswriting? As several of the journalists in this book point out, in a time when readers are confronted with a variety of things to do with their time, newspapers must present stories interestingly. A study by Lewis Donohew (1982) found that the narrative style of newswriting received higher reader attention and greater readership. Greater competition has created opportunities for literary newswriters in daily news work.

ELEMENTS OF THE LITERARY FEATURE

No reporter can just sit down and write a literary feature. It helps to know some of the elements of features and literary techniques.

The feature story is about people, and one of the first distinguishing characteristics of the standard feature is the use of the *anecdote*. The anecdote is to the feature what the inverted pyramid is to the hard news story. An anecdote can illuminate a point. Norman Cousins (1983), a successful magazine editor and author of several books, said:

> "The writer makes his living by anecdotes. He searches them out and craves them as the raw materials of his profession. No hunter stalking his prey is more alert to the presence of his quarry than a writer looking for small incidents that cast a strong light on human behavior. . . . To the writer, the universe itself begins with a single case, a single emotion, a single encounter—in short, a single person (p. 140)

Anecdotes are also useful in literary feature writing. But the literary feature writer must also consider a variety of techniques and elements. Among them are narration; point of view; scene; verb tense; process; drama; relevant detail; rhetorical devices such as metaphor and irony, mood, perspective, feel, type of news event, chronology, dialogue, foreshadowing and flashback; scene markers; and writing style.

What the literary feature writer attempts to do is write the first rough draft of history using literary techniques to create an interesting story for readers. As John Hersey (1949) once wrote: "Journalism allows its readers to witness history; fiction gives the readers an opportunity to live it" (p. 82). Literary feature writing can accomplish both.

The literary feature writer, then, seeks realism by melding the craft of reporting (i.e., getting the facts), the art of writing, and the techniques of fiction writing. Here are some of the ingredients of literary features.

Narrative

In simplest terms, a narration is an account of something. It is a story. A story comes with a storyteller—not someone in the story, but someone usually "outside" the story—the writer of the story. That is enough to distinguish it from typical journalistic writing, which contains internal sources and internal storytellers. Such sources are the people and documents to whom information is attributed.

For example, this lead: The president announced today that he is nominating a long-time political friend to head the Federal Trade Commission.

In that example, the internal source is the president. The rest of the story might contain information attributed to friends and opponents of the nominee. It might also cite written documents. The reporter is putting together the information and the sources into a readable news story, functioning more like a scribe than a storyteller.

The reporter who uses narrative must do the type of reporting/research that enables the reporter to write with authority. This is the "authority of fact" mentioned in the Introduction. One example of the narrative approach appears in Donald C. Drake's story (see chapter 4). Here are the first three paragraphs.

> It was a sunny Sunday afternoon. Washington's cherry blossoms had just begun their annual bloom. Tourists walked past the White House. Two blocks away, at the Park Central—a quiet, small hotel across the street from the headquarters of the Secret Service—a blond young man, unshaven and looking worn out, arrived a little before 1. The young man had just finished an exhausting three-day odyssey by bus across America from California.
>
> He walked through a small lobby and checked in, paying $47 in advance because he had not made a reservation. He went to Room 312, a small, comfortably furnished room that opened onto an inner courtyard.
>
> He carried with him a suitcase, a $47 handgun and a letter describing how he intended to assassinate the President of the United States.

Drake crafted a narrative from the reporting of 13 people. But a reporter who witnesses something happening can also be the source of information. That is the case with Richard Ben Cramer's story about the funeral of an Egyptian leader (see chapter 3). Here is the opening of Cramer's story, his narrative developed from his own reporting.

> CAIRO—Just minutes before the funeral, the people were walking on the airport road, past the soldiers and police with their submachine guns, past the sentries with their dogs.
>
> The people walked in a loose line, several thousand in a ragged file about half a mile long. Many carried newspaper photographs of Anwar Sadat or color posters ripped from six-cent magazines. The young men in their blue jeans carried slim, leafy branches, in the old Egyptian custom, as a mark of love, a symbol of peace, a funerary offering.

A major point needs to be stressed. Using the narrative is not simply a matter of not using attribution tags; the reporter must become an authority in his own right before he can become a storyteller. Reporting underlines the technique.

Point of View

For the journalist, literary point of view means deciding from which person's perspective a story is told. Usually, that is the central character. In fact, a story can lack impact when told from the wrong person's point of view.

Imagine this: A coach paces anxiously around the school's parking lot waiting for three of his star players to arrive for the 7 p.m. departure for a game in a nearby town. The stars do not show, and the coach decides to leave without them.

So far, the writer might want to tell the story from the coach's point of view. The writer would show the coach's anxiety and the story would continue throughout from the coach's point of view. But what if the stars were late because they were in an automobile accident? Perhaps, then, the story should be told from their point of view. They are the central characters and the ones most affected by the event.

In fact, what really happened was that the stars were in an auto accident and two of them were killed. In fact, the writer of the story attempted a literary bent by writing the story from the coach's point of view before lapsing into standard obituary information about the stars. In fact, the story failed because it was told from the "wrong" point of view. The reader has difficulty identifying with a high school coach's anxieties about late players when the real story is the death of two of them. So point of view is not something to be chosen lightly.

When John M. Crewdson was looking for a way of telling the story of illegal aliens, he chose as his central character an older man who had made many border crossings and who was experienced in the procedure (see chapter 9). Crewdson could have chosen a border patrol agent and told the story of illegal immigration from his point of view, but that would not have helped the reader understand illegal aliens, just a patrol agent's view of illegal aliens.

Scene

The more a writer shows a story happening the more the writer can compel a reader to read on. The reader gets more involved. Showing is achieved by relying on scene over summary. Here is one summary John Shinoff could have used to begin "A job where 'nobody complains' " (see chapter 5):

> John Fitzpatrick and Maurice Hickey begin their jobs as gravediggers at Holy Cross Cemetery at the crack of dawn [note cliche]. They know which gravesite to begin work at because their assignments are written on a piece of yellow paper Fitzpatrick has in his pocket.

That is a summary. This is how Shinoff really wrote the lead. He set the scene.

> The early-morning sun had barely cleared the top of the San Bruno mountains as John Fitzpatrick and Maurice Hickey trudged across the wet, well-manicured lawn of Holy Cross Cemetery, carrying shovels and spades.
> Fitzpatrick paused, took a folded yellow slip of paper from the pocket of his faded blue overalls and glanced at the name on the marble headstone.

Shinoff acts as the narrator of the story. In addition to showing scenes, he also shows the process of something happening rather than a summary of the process. The result is a more interesting story because the reader is made part of the action, part of the scene.

Another effective way of pulling the reader into the scene is to write in the present tense. Consider Shinoff's lead rewritten in the present tense:

> The early-morning sun has barely cleared the top of the San Bruno mountains as John Fizpatrick and Maurice Hickey trudge across the wet, well-manicured lawn of Holy Cross Cemetry, carrying shovels and spades.
> Fitzpatrick pauses, takes a folded yellow slip of paper from the pocket of his faded blue overalls and glances at the name on the marble headstone.

Ben Yagoda (1986) argued that using the present tense enables the writer, "in the TV age of shortened attention spans" (p. 50), to keep the reader's interest.[1] He sees the use of present tense as approximating television and movies, of making the printed word easier to read. Mike Sager, whose story appears in chapter 6, uses the present tense to good effect.

Ideally, the process approach bares the facts for the reader to interpret, but it may also prolong a small point in a story. Thus, a literary feature deviates from the literary mode by using summary or exposition when it can tighten a story or make a secondary point quickly or give context to the main point. That could include the need for several paragraphs of background. Crewdson turns to summary when he inserts some history on the Mexican village of Ahuacatlan. Summary is necessary when the reporting dictates that approach. Function decides form.

---

[1]Although not billed as such, "A Failing Grade for the Present Tense" by William H. Gass in the October 11, 1987, *New York Times Book Review* serves as a rebuttal.

The How of a News Event

The narrative approach to newspaper writing offers the journalist an opportunity to enhance the story's usefulness to the reader. Telling how something happened can provide insight for the reader and result in a better story. Usually, journalists attempt to learn everything they can about a news event. That includes the *what* of a story, that is, its importance. But for the journalist, the *what* of any news event can be a fuzzy theme that does not emerge in a daily context. Telling *how* some news event unfolded is an important part of journalism and adapting a literary technique to tell it does not diminish the journalist or the writing.

A good literary feature can be developed chronologically. Chronology can be used effectively to organize a literary feature, especially if the writer treats the event as unfolding rather than past, that is, writes in scenes rather than summary. As the writer attempts to describe the *how* of a news event, the implication always is that the journalist is also showing cause and effect. Frequently, however, that judgment—especially in the reconstruction of a news event—is difficult to make. The chronological pattern removes the burden of proof from the writer and puts it on the event. If the event does not show cause and effect, so be it.

Of particular relevance to this point is Donald C. Drake's story on the attempted assassination of President Reagan (see chapter 4). Drake traces the steps of the assassin, John W. Hinckley Jr., in the few days leading up to the attempt, not trying to say this is *why* the assassin acted as he did but more to show *how* he acted. The story provides insight on the assassin and his family.

Drama

Drake also takes advantage of drama. Part of the drama comes not from the event but from the telling. Drake uses film techniques to tell the story of Hinckley. Drake builds a scene then cuts to another. The reader must continue on to learn what happens. Notice how Drake creates tension with his lead.

Drake's story is a plotless narrative that shows a particular person at a particular juncture in his life. In literary feature writing, *plot* means *theme* or *topic*, and journalists control it only in the way they organize their stories, not by altering content. As Franklin (1987) puts it: "The most powerful techniques are useful only when they are harnessed in service of rigorous, factual honesty" (p. 13).

Literary newswriters put drama into their stories by the way they arrange their information into scenes. Tension is achieved in the way they present the information, not necessarily in the information itself. Literary newswriters do not fudge the facts for effect.

Scene Markers

Not every story flows neatly along. Sometimes the scene that would provide the ideal transition is missing. Other times the writer prefers abrupt cuts to new scenes, either as a way of building drama or of changing time.

Drake effectively breaks his story into scenes by using bullets. In his case, a bullet is a single dot between scenes. Other newspapers use different typographical devices. Paul Shinoff of *The San Francisco Examiner* uses three stars.

Note that in both cases, what appears between the breaks is related. The breaks do not interrupt the flow of a scene. Shinoff, for example, uses his breaks to shift from the scene at the graveyard to exposition on the history of cemeteries in San Francisco. Drake also uses his breaks to signal exposition. But because his story depends more on developing drama, Drake plotted his story as a series of scenes and then wrote each one. The bullets signal scene changes.

Transition

Some writers might consider space breaks a form of transition. But a space break tends to be abrupt, whereas transition is a smooth, almost imperceptible shift. In a compact story, a writer must produce smooth transitions.

Doris Wolf's sidebar on the funeral of a policeman provides examples of good transition (see chapter 2). She is writing about an event that occurs in three places—outside a funeral home, inside the funeral home, and at a cemetery. She moves back and forth through the use of simple transition sentences or paragraphs.

She opens her story by describing the many police officers who have shown up for the funeral. She uses one sentence that both describes the scene and enables her to shift the scene. This is how she shifts from outside the funeral home to inside.

> The officers formed silent ranks in the street, and at a shout from their commander turned, row by row, to march into the funeral parlor and past the open casket.
> Robert Van Hall laid at rest, a folded American flag at this head, a green beret from his service with the Army's Special Forces in Vietnam at his chest. At his feet was a heart-shaped spray of red and white flowers.

To get back outside, she relies again on the movement of the mourners through the line.

> Once or twice a man would move out of line and into a seat to sit for just a moment. But mostly they walked briskly back into the outside world. The walk in and out took just one minute, but it wasn't the time that mattered.
> A small crowd waited on the sidewalks outside the funeral home . . .

Wolf makes the transition to the cemetery by using the cortege.

> The cortege was five miles long as it traveled from the funeral home to the cemetery, the police cars with lights flashing, sirens silent.

Wolf makes effective use of events to aid her in transition. Instead of doing what she did, she could have shifted to inside the funeral home by beginning a paragraph with "Inside, Robert Van Hall laid at rest . . ." Then when she wanted to go out-side, she could have said: "Outside, a small crowd waited . . ." Both phrases would have worked, but they would have diminished Wolf's overall literary effect.

Relevant Detail

Wolf and others are aware of the need to put relevant detail into their stories. In writing a literary feature, journalists may not only use adjectives and adverbs, they may need them to create the accurate detail that puts a reader into a story. Detail in any good piece of journalism must be relevant. What is relevant? Examples abound. A reporter once wrote a story about a coal miner who chain smoked. That is not necessarily a relevant detail unless the reporter also revealed that the miner suffered from black lung disease, which smoking aggravates. Some detail reveals a person's status or lifestyle, such as reporting that as the subject of a story speaks, a grand-father clock chimes in the background. That detail reveals more when the reporter also notes that the subject of the story is deaf and cannot hear the chiming of her grandfather clock. Good detail creates concrete images for the reader and leaves the reader with a visual sense of the story.

One paragraph already cited in Wolf's story demonstrates her reliance on detail. That paragraph describes the dead narcotics investigator in his casket. Wolf pro-vides many details of the funeral, including this from the cemetery:

> The green and white-striped tent under which the commital service took place was pitched in front of leafless gray birches and a large green hemlock bush separating a swamp from the grassy graves.
> The flat stones on either side read "Suttelberg" and "Gloria Campbell."

Relevant detail allows the reader to see what is happening. Relevant detail can add a visual or perceptual dimension. Who needs television?

Dialogue

A lot of writing could be improved if writers relied less on direct quotations and more on paraphrasing what people say. That is because the good writer can usually write better than quoting a spontaneous remark, a remark that is seldom pithy and is probably wordy. Of course, direct quotations are invaluable when they make a point about a character in a story. For example, Richard Ben Cramer ends his story on the funeral of Anwar Sadat with a direct quotation intended to leave a lasting impression. (see chapter 3) Here is the final paragraph:

> The grandmother beat her hand softly up and down on the arm of the chair. She said: "O God, O God, help Egypt, Egypt."

Otherwise, direct quotations can impede the narrative flow, especially when they are used to provide biographical or other factual information that the writer could more easily summarize. The diminished role of direct quotations seems to fly in the face of one tenet of newspaper writing, which calls for a lot of "good quotes." But even good news stories do not read well when direct quotations provide background rather than color.

Cramer and other journalists published herein use dialogue effectively. Dialogue adds a dimension of realism to a story because it enables the reader to "hear" people talking. Dialogue gives us the voice of the characters in the story. Gilbert Gaul allows the Kintzel brothers their own voice by providing the reader with some dialogue (see chapter 7).

> When he is questioned about this, Kintzel retreats slightly but holds to his basic premise. "I have no proof of this exactly. But if you look at what's happening, I believe you'll see a pattern. The only ones going out of business are the independents, the small guys, while the big operators just seem to be getting richer and richer. I don't believe that's by accident either."
>
> "Like you said before, we're easy targets," Nathan assures his brother.
>
> "Nobody cares about the independents," Jesse murmurs.
>
> "It's a conspiracy is what I think—put all of your eggs in one basket," Nathan says.
>
> "If you ask me, it's true," Harvey nods in agreement.

Here is another example of the good use of dialogue. This comes from a *New York Times* (Malcolm, 1986) story titled "Fateful Choice in Fatal Illness: How Long to Live." It is the story of a man who upon learning he has cancer chooses to die at home rather than battle the uphill odds in a hospital. The reporter listens in as the doctor breaks the news:

> "Now why did this happen?" asked the doctor. "There are many holes in your bones. Some of your ribs are broken. There are lumps on your kidneys and bladder and lungs. These are tumors. And they're spreading. You kind of thought that, didn't you?"
>
> Mr. Anderson nodded.
>
> "Can we do anything?" the doctor continued. "Maybe. We don't know yet what kind of tumors these are. There are hundreds of kinds. A few respond to treatment. Some go away." He paused. "Others we can't do much about."
>
> He paused again. "We'll be very honest with you about the outlook," he went on. "But I won't have all the information for a day or so. Any questions?"
>
> "No."
>
> "You knew it?"
>
> "Yup. Keep right on it, Doc."
>
> "I will, but—are you a football fan?—well, it's fourth down, Mr. Anderson."
>
> "Thank you very much, doctor."
>
> "I don't know," the doctor said softly, "if 'thank you' is the right thing to say."
>
> "What did you say, Doc?"
>
> "Nothing," said Dr. Freeman. "I'll be back later."

Allowing the reader to listen in to this most intimate of conversations gives the story additional credibility.

Foreshadowing and Flashback

One effective device a writer can use is to suggest to the reader what is going to happen, to foreshadow events. After all, the writer who does not foreshadow does not help the reader, for without foreshadowing the reader does not know what is going to happen and has no reason to continue reading the story.

Donald C. Drake foreshadowed his story within three paragraphs of beginning it when he wrote:

> He carried with him a suitcase, a $47 handgun and a letter describing how he intended to assassinate the President of the United States.

Now the reader knows what the story is about and will continue reading to see *how* the main character in the story completes the foreshadowed action.

Another useful storytelling device is the flashback. The flashback allows the writer to go back in time, pick up a related thread in the story and fill in with relevant background material. The flashback becomes necessary as the story becomes more complex.

Drake also uses flashbacks in his story. For the most part, the story has dwelled on Hinckley's recent past. But on several occasions, Drake must reach farther back to help us understand Hinckley. Drake does this with flashbacks—and each flashback occurs at a bullet.

So, as the story unfolds primarily in the week leading up to the assassination attempt, Drake flashes back:

> Last November, one of the biggest majorities that Ronald Reagan received in his bid for the presidency was rolled up in a well-to-do area outside Dallas called Park Cities. It was there that John Warnock Hinckley Sr. became a millionaire oilman, a devout Christian who attends a weekly Bible-reading club and a devotee of the politics of Ronald Reagan. And it was there that John Warnock Hinckley Jr. was raised.

With that paragraph, Drake takes the reader back to Hinckley's childhood. The story moves on and eventually Drake is writing about Hinckley's current home in Evergreen, Colorado. But he must return to the past to explain more about Hinckley. So he turns to the flashback.

> On March 11, 1978, Michael C. Allen was preparing for the celebration of the 60th anniversary of the birth of the late George Lincoln Rockwell, founder of the American Nazi Party. Allen, then leader of the St. Louis section of the National Socialist Party, greeted 100 or so neo-Nazis and supporters gathering in party headquarters prior to a motorcade. A young sandy-haired man came up to him.

Allen was surprised, he remembers, that he didn't recognize someone clad in complete Nazi stormtrooper regalia—brown work shirt, belt ensemble, swastika armband, military trousers and jackboots. The young man said he was John Hinckley and wanted to join the party.

For the next eight paragraphs Drake explains Hinckley's affiliation with the American Nazi Party, ending the section by revealing that Hinckley's party membership was not renewed because of his radical beliefs.

Flashbacks enable Drake to give background late in the story and at a point where the information helps the reader understand the larger story. Flashbacks function as pieces of the puzzle that the writer is putting together for the reader. In that way, flashbacks add drama and tension to the story.

Other Elements

Any rhetorical device is allowed, and metaphor seems particularly useful in making a complex point simple. Gaul uses a mountain as a metaphor for a bureaucracy in "A fire on the mountain: The story of the Kintzel Brothers" (chapter 8).

Because some literary feature writers take the role of a narrator, they may use irony, but it must evolve naturally from events and cannot be used for its own sake lest the reporter's neutral role be open to challenge. Irony emerges in several stories, including Cramer's story on the funeral of Anwar Sadat. The entire story is ironic as Cramer shows the number of common people who want to attend Sadat's funeral and reports on the offical efforts to keep the common people away.

Literary features also leave room for first-person narration. That does not mean advocacy journalism. It means letting the reader know that the reporter is part of the story. That is what Gaul does, but he does it sparingly to avoid being intrusive. He begins his story this way:

> On a rinsed cobalt blue morning, Harvey Kintzel and I climbed aboard his 1973 Ford pickup and started up a winding dirt road into the small coalhole he and his three brothers have scraped a living from for the last 23 years.

Excessive first person fails because it makes the story unfold around the journalist rather than the real subject. Generally, newspaper editors oppose the use of first person outside the editorial page. Gaul's story began as a magazine piece and his editor retained that flavor when it was finally published in a newspaper.

Style of writing also helps distinguish the literary feature. The writer's style is the original way he or she brings words together. The writer's style is, in part, an attitude toward writing. A good writing style results in clear sentences propelled by strong verbs. Part of what makes a feature lies in the writing, in the ability of a reporter to recognize a set of facts that can be interestingly shaped. That does not mean writing with ruffles and flourishes and overstatement. But is does mean applying a style that raises the result above the mundane. Each story in this book is well written and far above the mundane. One writer, however, who might be cited as a stylist is Mike Sager of *The Washington Post*. Here is the beginning of Sager's piece:

> The dawn is chill inside the barn, and Greg Smith's breath hangs in the air like puffs from a hand-rolled smoke. A Hosltein stands motionless before him, and he strokes the cow's black and white face with a rough, stained hand. A few steps away, the sun outlines the open barn door on the earth and there summer lingers, warm to the skin.

Later on:

> The sun is round and low, and light splashes now across the fields more like a spreading coat of varnish than summer's sheer garment of translucent silk. Soon, the cows will linger in the barn, favoring the warmth of their extra winter issue of straw and sawdust over the cool grass by the pond, shadowed in the afternoon by Mount Pony.

The writing is original, descriptive and strong. It is Sager's style to write that way. Style is the sum of a writer.

Beginnings and endings need special care. The literary feature does not begin just anywhere that the writer feels like starting it. The opening must be compelling and relevant to the story. For example, Patricia Donahue's story about an abused child opens with a murder (see chapter 8):

> Larry hit her. And again. Faye fell over the coffee table onto the floor. He grabbed her neck and began choking her, but his grip was weak. The beer had left him unsteady and she broke away.
>
> "Go in there," he shouted, pointing to the bedroom. "And take your clothes off." His words confused her. Sex was the last thing Larry wanted when they fought. She thought perhaps he planned to put her out on the street naked.
>
> She started through the kitchen to the bedroom and caught sight of the claw hammer on the shelf by the sink. She grabbed it and turned. "Larry, don't hit me no more," she said.
>
> Bam! The blow to the side of her head was quick. Stunned momentarily, she raised the hammer in her right hand and backed Larry into the living room, into the arm of the red velour love seat.
>
> "Larry, don't hit me no more," she screamed. He hit her again, this time on the left temple.
>
> The hammer fell. Larry fell. Blood leapt from the left side of his head, onto the yellow curtains, onto the love seat, onto the brown and yellow shag carpet.
>
> The hammer fell four more times. Blood was everywhere. It was a crazy feeling. She sensed the finality to what she was doing, but she didn't stop. Turning the hammer around she hit him four more times, tearing chunks from his neck.

As you will learn in chapter 8, Donahue had a different beginning then realized that this one was the one that would draw the reader.

The ending must flow logically from the facts. A literary feature is strong if it does more than stop. Donahue knew that when she was working on the ending of her story. She wanted people to realize that the abused woman, a convicted murderer, remains abused and hurt. Here are the last three paragraphs:

> Her words come slowly as she thinks about the man she killed.
> I probably could kill somebody else. The first time was hard.
> The second time—a little easier.
> Probably could put a little more thought into it, too.

The ending is as compelling as the beginning.

Story type plays a part in literary features, primarily for the reporter who approaches an event with a literary intent. As Carol McCabe (Clark, 1980) of the *Providence* (Rhode Island) *Journal-Bulletin* put it: ''There are essentially very few [new] stories in fiction or in journalism. We're telling them over and over again. We're telling the story of life fighting death'' (p. 120). Not every story type lends itself to literary treatment. A congressional hearing demands straightforward reporting (if not recording) and would not make a good literary feature. However, keying on the role of one member of Congress in that hearing could make a good literary feature. A story about a retired railroader who raises prize-winning gladioli is worth a 2½ page feature with one or two pictures, but he is probably not worth 10 pages of narrative. So, although a literary feature will focus on people rather than topics, not every person lends himself to literary treatment. The perceived impact of the event that focuses on a person no doubt contributes to the thinking that goes on before editors and reporters decide the form of the story. If the material for a literary feature does not exist, a writer cannot fake it.

TEN STEPS
IN THE WRITING PROCESS

Using several literary techniques and rhetorical devices does not mean a story will succeed as literary writing. More than mere devices are needed to fashion a literary feature. The writing must be good. One of the best ways to understand writing is to break it down into its many steps. Once isolated and presented sequentially, the steps show how each one depends on the preceding. Missing one or not doing one right can have a negative effect on the following steps.

- The first step is reporting.

No journalist can write about nothing or make something out of thin air. No journalist can fashion a literary feature without doing a tremendous amount of reporting, of gathering mounds and mounds of information that the journalist might otherwise ignore in the standard news story. A successful story cannot be based on one source. One has to marvel at not only the time the journalists in this book spent reporting their stories, but also the intensity of their efforts.

When Carol McCabe was asked how she reconciled reporting and writing, she told Roy Peter Clark (1980) in *Best Newspaper Writing 1980*: "It's the reporting that underlines the good writing. You've got to have the basic facts to build on, and then you work with language in a way that makes it not 'fancier'—I like 'plainer'" (p. 116).

• The second step is thinking.

I call this *analysis aforethought*. And I must admit that it is really not a step, but a continuum. A good writer is always thinking, regardless of what stage the writing is at.

Those who do not write against a daily deadline find many ways to think about their writing. Some people go for long walks; others jog. I know of a sportswriter who talks to his taperecorder as he drives back from an event. It helps him think through the story so that when he reaches the newsroom, he's ready to write. And, no, he does not play back the tape. It's just there if he needs it.

So, whatever the method, most writers make the time to think about what they're going to say. Usually, they write better.

• The third step is organization.

That is, how well the writer organizes stories before beginning to write. Although outlines may sound burdensome to a writer, the fact remains that the writer who loses time in outlining makes it up in writing. An organized writer can write faster and better. An organized writer knows where the story has been and where it is going. Although some novice writers may believe that after they put down the first sentence, a story writes itself, most writers find that a story writes itself only after the writer plans it.

Charlie Chaplin once asked Igor Stravinsky: "How do you know when to end a composition?" Stravinsky replied: "Before I begin."

The most natural way to organize facts is logically. Keep related facts together; put one fact after another in a logical way. Put good detail into the body, and wherever possible, show, don't tell. Good examples strengthen any piece of writing.

Several stories in this book show strict organization schemes, especially the longer ones. Donald Drake's is an example. He organized his story around a series of scenes, some of which foreshadowed events, others of which flashbacked to provide history.

• The fourth step is mechanics.

A good writer gets the mechanics right because that is what the audience understands. The mechanics of our language are conventions, and the writer follows the conventions of his audience—standard punctuation and grammar. Nothing idiosyncratic. Who would understand?

In ancient times, one history says, "Correct Greek or Latin was regarded as the first virtue in writing." And, in fact, we owe most punctuation to the Romans, who used it to keep their words from bumping together and becoming meaningless. The mechanics have been with us for a long time. It is not something invented by ninth-grade English teachers to harass students.

- The fifth step is style.

Style is the flavor, quality, spirit, and personality of a written piece. Style is the sum of a writer. In part, it is an attitude: A good writer wants to write well and interestingly and to use original language. Avoid cliches. Avoid jargon. Write it as it has never been written before. Be original.

- The next three steps form the story.

They are the lead, the body and the ending. Together they represent what unity a story has. If they are not connected, the story lacks unity.

- The lead or first paragraph—step six—needs to engage the reader.

Leads can be of various types—shocking statement, narrative, descriptive, summary, informative, direct address, quote, question, surprise, teaser, and so on—but what the writer should really appreciate about a lead is that it should be determined by the content. Don't decide to write a particular lead because it is the middle of the month and it is time for such a lead; write a lead that comes naturally from the information you have gathered.

- Step seven is the body.

This is where the seed of good reporting grows. If the reporter has failed to gather enough or the right information, the body of the story will suffer. If the reporter fails to organize the facts, the body of the story will suffer. It is in the body where the writer focuses the story.

- Step eight is the ending.

Knowing when to stop is important. The impact of a story that continues beyond its natural conclusion is diluted because the reader senses entrapment rather than enlightenment.

The story should conclude naturally, not with some pious summary by the writer but with a bold fact that continues the feeling of the story beyond the page it appears on and beyond the moment it was read.

- Step nine is evaluation.

A good writer is also a good editor, as difficult as that task is when you are editing your own work. Editing your own copy is almost like disciplining your own children. My children are perfect. How could my creations need improvement!

Well, we all know better.

Writing is discovery, and most discoveries are made in the evaluation stage. Those who do not evaluate their own writing do not discover much from having written it.

One important test in this stage is asking if the story lived up to its intention. If not, perhaps rewriting or re-reporting is necessary.

Another thing you might discover in this stage is what art or other graphic might go with the story to help you tell it.

- Step ten is the rewriting and re-reporting stage.

Of course, every piece of writing can benefit from rewriting. Rewriting allows a writer to focus a story more sharply. In re-reporting, a writer fills in the holes.

Writing is hard work. It is not like memorizing multiplication tables. Once you know them, you are over the hump. Two times two is always four.

Once done, writing does not get easier the next time you do it. Those who write clearly do toil. But the good result that comes from hard work is worth it. Excellence is its own reward.

Chapter Two
It Was a Day the Brave Men Cried

BACKGROUND

This is the story of the funeral of a New York State police officer who was killed while serving as an undercover narcotics investigator. He was the first trooper in 5 years to be killed in the line of duty. Doris Wolf, of the *Finger Lakes Times* in Geneva, New York, was assigned to cover the funeral. She spent 8 hours covering the funeral then wrote two stories—the funeral for page one and a sidebar, which is reprinted here. Prior to the funeral, she had been told "that a cop's funeral would be an intense emotional experience, and I had 'tuned up' all of my senses, ready to absorb as much detail as I could. Coming upon the funeral scene and seeing the massed battalions of policemen standing in the street set the tone of the day." Instead of standing in one place, Wolf wandered about. "My editor always seems to have a question about the one thing I didn't include and I wanted to be sure I observed every detail." She watched the police officers file past the open casket. "I looked carefully at their faces. I wanted to see why these men came, what this experience meant to them, so I could put some meaning into it for those who weren't there." She also talked to some of the police officers outside the funeral home. Then she returned home. "The experiencing was done on one day, and the story put on paper the next."

BIOGRAPHY

Doris Wolf graduated from Boston University where she double majored in political science and journalism. She interned with the Associated Press in Washington,

DC, and the *Berkshire Eagle* in Pittsfield, Massachusetts. She worked for a public relations firm in Boston for 8 years and also did free-lance public relations work. When her husband became a professor at Colgate University in Hamilton, New York, she went to work as a stringer for newspapers and a radio station in Norwich and Oneida. She also worked as a grant proposal writer and demonstrator/teacher. Her husband then joined the faculty at Eisenhower College and Wolf became a stringer for the *Finger Lakes Times*. She also worked in public relations for a direct selling jewelry company for 18 months before becoming a member of the *Times'* staff.

THE STORY

It was a day the brave men cried

BY DORIS WOLF

BUFFALO—It was a day the brave men cried.

They came, almost 3,000 of them, to salute a fallen comrade, a man some had worked or trained with, but most never knew.

It was enough that he wore the uniform.

They came to bear witness to undercover narcotics investigator Robert Van Hall, a former Waterloo and Geneva area resident who was killed in a shotgun blast while on a drug investigation in Corning Friday night.

The men wore the somber gray uniforms of the New York State Police, the blue of the Massachusetts State Police, the high brown leather laced up boots of the Rhode Island troopers, the crimson red jackets of the Royal Canadian Mounted Police, the earthy brown of the N.Y. State Department of Environmental Conservation. They wore shoulder patches that read California, Illinois, Toronto, and Border Patrol.

Their badges, silver or gold shield or stars, were bisected with strips of black tape in official mourning.

The uniformed police stood in sharp contrast to Van Hall's fellow plainclothesmen, who wore beards, mustaches and trench coats.

"He had a job to do and he did it," Investigator Edward McGuigan, a Geneva police-man said. "He didn't seek recognition in his work. This is one of the ways we can say how much we respected him."

Buffalo police estimated there were almost 700 police cars parked in the 10-block area along Bailey Avenue where the funeral was held. The men from Troop E in Canandaigua came by four buses, parked opposite the Carlton Ullrich Funeral Home.

The officers formed silent ranks in the street, and at a shout from their commander turned, row by row, to march into the funeral parlor and past the open casket.

Robert Van Hall laid at rest, a folded American flag at his head, a green beret from his service with the Army's Special Forces in Vietnam at his chest. At his feet was a heart-shaped spray of red and white flowers.

Resting on the edge of the upturned lid of the green metal coffin was a red and white spray which bore the word "Husband" on its red ribbon. Troopers stood at parade rest at the head and foot, facing the family and staring straight ahead.

Some 30 large baskets of flowers lined the room where friends sat in silent tribute.

Organist Geraldine Bork played "Onward Christian Soldiers" as the men filed in and out, past the white Christmas tree trimmed in red satin balls and velvet ribbons which stood in one corner of the red brocaded anteroom. As the men left, they passed Mrs. Bork and the strangely gay animated holiday figures beside the organ—a man tipping his top hat, a holiday-dressed woman pulling on a silent white bell.

The procession of troopers halted and Gov. Hugh Carey entered, paused at the bier, and said a few words to the family. Then he took a seat on the left of the aisle, and the long line started filing past once more.

Now it was the Bureau of Criminal Investigation men, their expressions barely changing as they marched by, one biting his lip, one carrying his hat over his heart, one with his hand over his heart in silent salute.

Older men glanced at Van Hall as they passed, and continued, blinking hard. Younger men, some of those with the beards, looked down, or to the side, as the moment came to face their own mortality. Occasionally a man would cross himself. One stepped out of line and handed Mrs. Van Hall a Bible in a cedar box. There were only a few women, all red-eyed, who passed by in the ranks.

Once or twice a man would move out of line and into a seat to sit for just a moment.

But mostly they walked briskly back into the outside world. The walk in and out took just one minute, but it wasn't the time that mattered.

A small crowd waited on the sidewalks outside the funeral home, many former policemen. Former Erie County sheriff Mike Amico stood there, along with Buffalo police homicide chief Leo Donovan, a couple of men who said they had been cops on the Bailey Street beat, and a postal employee. Van Hall worked for the post office for two years. Retired cop Joe O'Brien spoke for them when he said he came "to thank God it wasn't me."

The cortege was five miles long as it traveled from the funeral home to the cemetery, the police cars with lights flashing, sirens silent.

The honor guard of state troopers and Green Berets lined the woven brown mat that stretched from the road to the grave. Behind them stood plainclothesmen and uniformed officers.

The green and white-striped tent under which the committal service took place was pitched in front of leafless gray briches and a large green hemlock bush separating a swamp from the grassy graves.

The flat stones on either side read "Suttelberg" and "Gloria Campbell."

"How many cars?" the plainclothesmen repeatedly asked a reporter. "What a wonderful tribute," they responded when told.

The head pallbearer, a member of Van Hall's four man narcotics squad, Ron Martin, delivered the eulogy, a personal statement of love, and humor, and tribute.

"And now, on behalf of the family, I'd like to express our appreciation for this tremendous tribute to Robert Van Hall . . ." Martin broke off, and turned, sobbing, to the arms of another pallbearer and fellow squad member.

Van Hall's daughter, Tracy, stiffened as the honor guard of Army men prepared to fire their salute, and his wife, Sandra, slumped forward as the shots exploded.

The eyes of a trooper standing at the foot of the coffin were damp as he began folding the flag, and tears were running down another's face when he handed the flag to Martin.

For one long moment, Martin clutched the flag to his heart, a final hug for the man whom he said was "more than a squad member . . . we were a family."

He bent to give the flag to Sandra Van Hall, with a kiss, and helped her stand and walk away.

"We have the best, and we have lost the best," Troop E commander Major Ralph Smith said in a final benediction.

And the honor guard remained at attention, eyes red and tear-filled, still at their posts, doing their jobs.

DISCUSSION

Some literary feature writers attempt to develop a sensory dimension of a news event, to go beyond a few observations and direct quotations. "What I do is try to experience fully a situation, using all my senses, and then translate that experience into words," Wolf says. "People often say they feel as if they've actually been there when they read a story I've written."

After she wrote the main story of the police officer's funeral, Wolf says "I sat back and wrote the 'feeling' of the event." She achieves feeling in a multitude of ways. She is particularly strong on description. She is specific about the number of police officers and police cars and the length of the funeral cortege. When she describes the colors of the many uniforms, she also contrasts the colors. Later, she contrasts the appearances of the uniformed police officers and the dead police officer's undercover colleagues. Wolf gives the name of the organist, which makes her an individual, not a function, and she notes minute details such as the mourning stripes on badges and the Christmas decorations inside the funeral parlor.

Because Wolf approaches an event with the intention of recreating the emotional experience for the reader, she is careful in her reporting and her writing. She almost understates the impact of the day's emotions by resorting to simple description.

Older men glanced at Van Hall as they passed, and continued, blinking hard.

She raises that line to a literary level with her next sentence.

Younger men, some of those with the beards, looked down or to the side, as the moment came to face their own mortality.

It is the ending of that sentence that helps set Wolf's prose off from standard reportage. Such a sentence could not stand in a typically written story. Because Wolf has done so well developing the style of this story, the phrase fits naturally. It does not call attention to itself.

Wolf's style is an effective use of simple words that combine to create a picture.

She thinks in pictures, but uses concrete language. For example, she could have finished the story this way:

> And the honor guard remained at attention, still at their posts, doing their jobs.

But she adds a concrete phrase to the sentence and provides a strong finish with words the reader can see.

> And the honor guard remained at attention, *eyes red and tear-filled*, still their posts, doing their jobs.

Because we have all cried and have seen others cry, we know the image.

Wolf does use an occasional figure of speech (''as the moment came to face their own mortality'' is the best example) and she does use adjectives. Adjectives and adverbs are not typical in standard newspaper writing because they can be evaluative. In literary feature writing, adjectives and adverbs help the journalist produce vivid pictures. Adjectives and adverbs help form a picture. Additionally, adjectives can result in more accurate writing. Accuracy is the backbone of good writing.

Wolf uses an adjective in her lead: ''It was a day the brave men cried.'' Without the word ''brave,'' the lead would lose meaning. ''It was a day the men cried'' lacks the contrast Wolf evokes when she says ''brave men cried.'' The reader may not analyze the contrast, but the point is made and the reader goes on.

Elsewhere, Wolf is particular about colors: somber gray uniforms, brown leather boots, silver or gold badges, white Christmas tree trimmed in red satin balls and velvet ribbons, red brocaded anteroom, and not just the red jackets of the Royal Canadian Mounted Police, but *crimson* red. Her desire to record every detail is not an uncommon trait among literary feature writers, and others in this book echo Wolf's creed on detailed reporting.

Because Wolf has done such a good job recreating the event, she gives the feeling that it is the actual thing. Wolf is restrained in her telling and that restraint lets the story come out on its own. ''The best stories, to use a cliche, write themselves,'' Wolf says. But she is being modest for she could have easily overwritten this story and spoiled the effect.

In general, this story can be blocked off into four parts—(a) purpose of story, (b) inside the funeral home, (c) outside the funeral home, (d) at the cemetry. The first few paragraphs establish the sense and mood—what the story is about. Wolf then uses a direct quotation to give one person's interpretation of the massive turn-out of police officers. She follows with a head count paragraph. Using the line of police officers as her transition, she takes the readers inside the funeral home, first describing the dead man and then the interior scene. But throughout this segment of the story, Wolf also continues to describe the reactions of the police officers moving through the line. After all, this story is Wolf's attempt at recording an intense emotional experience—that of living police officers at the funeral of one of their own.

The line of officers also serves as her transition to the outside and she closes with the committal service at the cemetery. And although Wolf mentions the widow and daughter, she closes by focusing on the police—the subjects of her story. They are the organizational thread of this story.

Wolf maintains a fairly chronological pattern and inserts description and background as needed. She quietly notes the ironies of life, that only 2 weeks before Christmas a young family is burying their husband and father. But Wolf never says that, choosing instead to describe the Christmas decorations and letting the reader do the rest.

Wolf also maintains an effective pace with long and short paragraphs. Her cadence starts slowly, builds in the middle of the story, and then slackens as the story and the funeral end. In a story like this, a journalist might be quick to gather many direct quotations and use them throughout the story. Wolf's story contains few direct quotations and those few she does have are (with one exception) remarks made in front of the mourners rather than to her. The story Wolf has written is about the funeral and not about Wolf covering the funeral. A lot of direct quotations would have interrupted this story's rhythm. Other examples of literary feature writing bear out the observation that a good story does not always need direct quotations to have human qualities. Such a story does need a good reporter and a good writer.

Chapter Three
Left Behind

BACKGROUND

The funeral for assassinated Egyptian president Anwar el-Sadat was attended by 800 leaders from 80 nations, including 3 former United States presidents. The *Philadelphia Inquirer* combined information from its wire services to provide the main coverage of the funeral, but relied on one of its international correspondents, Richard Ben Cramer, for special coverage. Cramer, who spent 20 hours reporting and writing, produced a story of Sadat's funeral as seen through the eyes of Egyptians who could not attend because their leaders kept them away. Cramer says he chose not to join the main body of journalists because they were kept together at one spot and got only one view. Cramer wanted the reaction of the common people. With his approach, he came up with a different point of view of the funeral. Cramer says he tries to develop the character of people in his reporting. He says he wants to hear people speaking. Because his editor is not in the room, Cramer says he reads his copy carefully and challenges unclear statements. He tries to anticipate his editor's questions about holes in his stories. He calls the approach "Scrooge reading," and says: "I try to come back at myself as though the editor were there."

BIOGRAPHY

Richard Ben Cramer is a 1971 graduate of Johns Hopkins University with a bachelor of arts degree in liberal arts. He received a masters degree in journalism from Columbia University in 1972, then for the next 4 years worked as a reporter for the Baltimore *Sun*. He left the *Sun* for the *Inquirer*, working first as its transportation writer then in its New York bureau before being sent to Cairo for the Christmas Day 1977 negotiations between Anwar el-Sadat, president of Egypt, and Menachim Begin, prime minister of Israel. Cramer remained as the *Inquirer*'s Middle East correspondent. Among his awards is a Pulitzer Prize in international reporting and an American Society of Newspaper Editors' award for good newswriting under deadline.

THE STORY

Left behind
The Egyptian people mourn apart

(Sunday, October 1, 1981. Reprinted with permission
from *The Philadelphia Inquirer*, 1981).

By Richard Ben Cramer
Inquirer Staff Writer

CAIRO—Just minutes before the funeral, the people were walking on the airport road, past the soldiers and police with their submachine guns, past the sentries with their dogs.

The people walked in a loose line; several thousand in a ragged file about half a mile long. Many carried newspaper photographs of Anwar Sadat or color posters ripped from six-cent magazines. The young men in their blue jeans carried slim, leafy branches, in the old Egyptian custom, as a mark of love, a symbol of peace, a funerary offering.

There were fathers holding their children, older men in traditional long cotton robes, schoolgirls walking hand in hand, older peasant women swaddled in gauzy black. These women rent the air with their cries:

"O my misfortune . . .

"O my plague . . .

"O leader of the nation . . .

"O my beloved . . ."

There was more than grief on their faces; there was urgency in their look, in their walk. They were tireless in the hot noon glare; they were searching, probing. They were heading for the funeral of their president, and they could not get in.

The buildings on the airport road had high walls running out to the street. The openings between were sealed by troops. For miles around the funeral, Egyptians searched for a way in toward the square and their hero. But this funeral was not for them.

No, Sadat was buried well away from the people he served, the people he called his family, "the family of Egypt." His successors ruled that family could not be trusted.

A swatch of concrete

He was buried far from his chosen plot—his planned "peace shrine" on Mount Sinai with a tomb for himself, the maker of peace, and a sanctuary for Muslims, Christians and Jews. His survivors decided he woud lie in the same swatch of concrete where he was gunned down Tuesday—a brutal, dirt-brown plaza in a Cairo suburb called by the warlike name, "Victory City."

He was buried in fly-flecked pomp, pre-packed for TV, bid farewell by cameramen and foreigners and a stiff retinue of officials who preside, now, in an Egypt already changed from the nation he ruled a week ago.

The people on the airport road couldn't believe it. A middle-aged man with a trim mustache rallied the rest in the quest for entry: "If the people stand together we'll get in. What is this? He's our leader, not theirs."

And they found a way. Near a road that led into "Victory City," a concrete wall had tumbled to ruin. Those in front scrambled over dirt hillocks and over a low fence onto the road behind the main police cordon.

Troops lined the feeder road, too. But they had no orders. They stood still, rigidly pointing their submachine guns at the citizens who streamed past them on to the road.

Near the back of the file, still on the airport road, a balding man watched gleefully as the line in front of him diminished and the line on the feeder road thickened. "They got in, the smart bastards." He cackled and made for the low fence, too. "Forward the people, forward," he called.

They were running now, straight for the square. And the line stretched longer and longer, thousands running: The women in black with their plastic sandals flopping called out, still half in grief, half in joy and release; children with the grim little faces of old men shot toward the head of the file. An old man was falling back. He grabbed the hem of his long robe, hiked it up and held it in his teeth while he ran with an eager stride for the tomb of Anwar Sadat.

•

"And although we are saying farewell to Sadat, the people of this country still cannot believe that Sadat is gone. . . . "

The commentator talked on while the big color TV screen showed again the flags flying and the soldiers at attention.

". . . And all the dignitaries today, still, we are sure, would like to think this is a bad dream from which they will wake up and find it was just a bad dream, a nightmare that passes and was not really true, so. . . . "

In his armchair, the grandfather grunted. "This man talks too much." The grandfather did not talk much, although he might have. He was a learned man, a sheik of some eminence. He knew Sadat, and liked him.

'They only wanted money'

"He was a good man." he said. "But some of the people around him were not good. They only wanted money."

The grandmother, in the next armchair, seemed a simpler soul. Her toes curled in furry slippers. She was thinking about lunch for the group. She said, absently, with her eyes on the screen, "I liked him."

Their daughter nodded and drew on her long American cigarette. She was a woman of some sophistication, just returned to Cairo from Paris. "It's a bad time," she said. "I never heard so many rumors."

The third generation of the family was absent. The young man had grown up with television; it held no fascination for him. He had grown up with Sadat, too; there, the fascination endured. He wanted to be close to the funeral, though barred from the square itself.

" . . . to the same reviewing stand where all the world saw, where all the world saw the dignity of this man, at the peak of his glory, looking up in full pride, with all his decorations as the bullets struck his chest. . . "

The call to prayer

Outside the living room window, the muezzin from the nearby mosque started the noon call to prayer.

On the screen, a drum tattoo began and black horses drew the caisson toward the square in "Victory City."

Then, the talk in the living room was spare:

"Who's that?"

"I don't know."

"Japanese."

"Where's Begin?"

From the television, the talk increased:

" . . . and the new president of the republic, uh, vice president, Hosni Mubarak, who, uh, has been nominated for the presidency and of course we will have the referendum on Tuesday. . . .

" . . . and everybody is here, apart from the millions, who. . . .

•

Now, the people were running down the feeder road, past the soldiers who pointed the guns held under the crook of their arms.

A man in a long gray gown shouted at the soldiers: "We are the people. Why are you pointing your guns at us? Do you have orders? Damn your orders!"

A soldier leaned toward the man in the gown. Solicitously, he took his left hand from under the barrel of his Kalashnikov rifle and placed it over his mouth.

"Uncle, uncle," he said to the man. "Please. Say no more. Just go."

Another man running toward the square said to the one in the long gray gown: "Shut up, you old fool. Do you think they like it? Six hours in the sun?"

Most of the crowd just ran by, down the road to "Victory City."

But 100 yards ahead, the front of the streaming file slowed up. Army and police had thrown up another cordon: trucks, jeeps, more soldiers, four lines of riot police armed with sticks and shields.

An officer took out his handgun and fired shots in the air. Still the people approached. The file was bunching up now, as those in the rear caught up.

For a frozen minute, in sun without shadow, the thousands stood in a silent clump while ahead the soldiers and riot police stood in silent rows.

On the left, the clump of people started to dissolve as those who were nearest made for a side street to try to outflank the cordon. A phalanx of white-coated city policemen ran to link hands and seal off the side street.

A strange silence

Then, almost without sound as their footfalls were muffled by dust, the riot police marched forward.

They marched till they got to the trapped ones in front and then they thrust American plastic shields and swung their billy clubs. Weird silence, as they beat the crowd back, a muffled scuffling as everybody tried to run at once, over the ones in back of them.

It was no fight. In the frightened center of the mob, there was only the chaotic muddle of flight, and behind, a vision of the helmeted rows, bobbing up and down as they shoved, their clubs leaping here and there along the line like some piston machine gone amok.

And then the silence broke. No one will ever know who started, but all at once the crowd was chanting in flight:

"There is no God but God, and Muhammed is his prophet."

These were not the militant Muslims who are blamed for Sadat's murder. They were simple folk who yelled the first thing they knew, the one they knew best.

One man who was in it tried later to explain:

"It gives you strength. It's the closest thing to your heart. If you know what it means, it helps you. Everything else is just emptiness."

•

On the screen, the camera panned again down the gold script on Sadat's gravestone. The script was a verse from the Koran:

"Those who die for the sake of God are not dead, they are at the side of the Almighty."

The grandfather said:

"When (Saudi Arabian King) Faisal died, he was buried in the desert. No signs, no stones, just like that."

"*. . . and whatever the conspiracies around us, Egypt will always pride herself on the unity of her national front, on the . . . "*

"This is not a funeral," the grandfather said, "No prayers, no Koran. What is this?"

The grandmother had a hankie in her hand.

"There's Jihan," she said. The camera lingered on Mrs. Sadat crying at the grave.

"Right in the spot where they killed him," said the grandmother. She wiped her eyes with her hankie.

The mother said, "This is unpleasant to watch this."

"*Oh, leader, here we are in your state, the state of security, of democracy, of the village morality. . . . "*

The son walked in the living room, carrying a bottle of water he had picked up in the kitchen on his way in.

He slumped in a chair and drained half the quart bottle. They looked at him expectantly. He wiped his mouth.

"Couldn't get close," he said. "Almost got beaten up."

•

The people had run from the police, who finally halted and abandoned their advance.

Most of the people escaped in ones and twos, disappearing into the side streets close to the airport road. Only one group was left, no more than 100 or 200, standing on the feeder road, well away from the lines of police.

Then the ranks parted and an open jeep roared out from behind the police lines. It sped at the crowd. A soldier was driving. Another soldier sat beside him. Two plainclothes men sat in the back.

The jeep braked sharply right in the middle of the people. Again, that curious dust-muffled silence: no tire squeal or brake whine. For a moment, the crowd scuffled and hid the jeep from view. It seemed these hundreds of people must engulf, overwhelm one car.

But the crowd scattered and the jeep roared back toward "Victory City." In the back, the plainclothes men were beating two men.

All at once, there was no crowd at all. Just a few people, who seemed not to know where to go.

Three girls in tight blue jeans and heavy makeup walked away. One said: "Let's go watch on TV."

A couple of others went nowhere at all. They sat down on the dust on the road. For them, the funeral was over.

•

"O leader, o martyr, o you who have fulfilled the duty, lie peacefully. . . . "
The mourners were standing in a knot while the grave was being closed on the screen. The camera showed Hosni Mubarak flicking a finger to direct workmen and soldiers.
The grandmother said, "They're asking Hosni Mubarak, now."
"Good," the grandfather said. "That's right."
The son said, "He's the boss, now."
"The king is dead," the mother said. "Long live the king." She left the room to go talk on the telephone.

"It is not up to Hosni Mubarak," the grandfather said. He was not watching the screen.

"It is up to the United States and Israel. If they go straight with him, he will do well.

"Reagan and Begin must go the straight way with him, or Mr. Hosni will go very, very quickly. Egypt is just waiting, waiting for one thing to go not straight. Then, the Egyptian people will change immediately all that Mr. Anwar has done. Immediately."

"Go forward, Egypt. The morrow that Sadat has created for you is yours only. For your generations to come. . . . "
In the other corner of the room, the son was telling the grandmother what he had seen on the street.

Her voice rose. She said, "But why, why?"

"I don't know," the young man said. "I've never seen Cairo like this. It seems to have changed. The streets are empty. No one around. No sound. And during the feast!"

"They are sad," the grandmother said.
"Scared," the grandfather said.
"I don't know," said the son. "Everything's changed."
The grandfather sat back and fell silent.
The grandmother beat her hand softly up an down on the arm of the chair. She said: "O God, O God, help Egypt, Egypt."

DISCUSSION

Richard Ben Cramer claims to have only two rules for good newspaper writing, the second of which is: "Stick with your senses. We all want readers to be active participants in the process of moving the news. We want them to imagine what it must be like there, to try to feel with us and our subjects what a story or a scene feels like. But readers, not unjustly, require some help to imagine: What does it smell like? Is it hot? How does the dust taste? Did that cafe have music? As long as I constantly refer to my basic senses while I'm reporting, I have a chance to put the reader there with me while he reads. When I neglect the senses, the writing lacks texture, the reader is left behind." For Cramer, the way to report is to describe in detail what happened, to be specific about everything. "If a yellow belly sapsucker lands on an apple tree," he says, "I don't say, 'A bird lands in a tree.'" Cramer avoids shortcuts. He tries to get people speaking so the reader can hear the people speaking. Cramer achieves that rather difficult task on deadline through a simple presentation that relies on a single evocative word, in this case, a verb.

In his armchair, the grandfather grunted. "This man talks too much."

Cramer could have devalued the sentence had he chosen a word other than "grunted." By using "grunted" and not "said" or another attributive, Cramer evokes in the reader the reader's own sense of a grandfather grunting.

Cramer also accomplishes something in his writing that is hard for a journalist on deadline to do—he gets inside the minds of many of the people in his stories and attempts to learn what motivates them. To do that, a journalist has to do a great deal of research. Cramer does that. He tries to develop a person's character, mostly through extensive interview. He limits himself to how many people he will interview so he can get depth rather than breadth. For this story, Cramer had access to the family the night before the funeral and his assistant is a friend of the family.

Throughout, Cramer gives glimpses of the family, beginning with the paragraph about the grandfather. In a few sentences, the reader learns that the grandfather knew Sadat and how the grandfather felt about the assassinated president. Immediately, Cramer gives a view of the grandmother, and because he at some point asked, he is able to tell the reader what is on the grandmother's mind. Then on to the daughter and to a grandson—three generations and three different views.

Cramer allows the reader to learn about the Egyptian family slowly, rather than in one neat section. Several scenes later, after having "seen" what is going on outside, at the funeral, and on television, the reader learns more about the family. This is a story of contrasts and it is the contrasts that serve as Cramer's organization scheme. In essence, the story consists of six major scenes—the crowd, then the family watching on television contrasted three times. The television commentator, his remarks italicized, links the contrasting scenes.

The shifting scenes provide irony and give the story the quality of a narrative film. The story comes through Cramer's controlled point of view. He sharpens his focus, then draws back. He provides some detail and context, focuses on another scene, then backs off. Cramer's story cuts from scene to scene, providing, despite the breaks, an impression of continuing action.

Cramer uses scene rather than summary to great benefit. Notice how he shows the crowd atempting to get to the funeral. Then the crowd is halted. It finds a new way, along a feeder road, and the reader has the impression, as Cramer cuts to the family for several paragraphs before going back to the crowd outside, that the crowd will reach the funeral site. Even when he cuts back to the crowd, it is still advancing along a feeder road and some soldiers seem willing to let the crowd through.

But 100 yards ahead, the front of the streaming file slowed up. Army and police had thrown up another cordon: trucks, jeeps, more soldiers, four lines of riot police armed with sticks and shields.

An officer took out his handgun and fired shots in the air. Still the people approached. The file was bunching up now, as those in the rear caught up.

For a frozen minute, in sun without shadow, the thousands stood in a silent clump while ahead the soldiers and riot police stood in silent rows.

On the left, the clump of people started to dissolve as those who were nearest made for a side street to try to outflank the cordon. A phalanx of white-coated city policemen ran to link hands and seal off the side street.

Then, almost without sound as their footfalls were muffled by dust, the riot police marched forward.

This scene, and an earlier one, allows the reader to see how the crowd attempted to frustrate the efforts of the authorities. By using scene, Cramer takes the reader with the crowd. The reader does not learn any sooner than the crowd about the outcome of the trip down the feeder road. By cutting back and forth, Cramer creates dramatic tension. Had Cramer used summary, he might have produced this paragraph:

A crowd of mourners attempted to reach the funeral site by ducking around a roadblock and taking a feeder road. But soldiers and city and riot appeared and cut short the crowd's advance.

Summary does not allow the reader to see the story unfold in continuing action. Scene does.

Cramer aims to get many views of the same event in his stories. To do that with this story he had an assistant, an Egyptian who began working for Cramer in 1977 as his interpreter. Cramer calls him a good reporter. He tells him what to watch for, then sends him to gather information. "If I tell him to vacuum a situation, he does," Cramer says. "He'll come back with a notebook filled with useful notes."

Cramer is very successful in getting emotion into the story. It is journalistic heresy to suggest that a news story can contain anything but fact, and typically one expects to find emotion only in fiction. But Cramer gets the two seemingly conflicting components of the narrative in his story—fact and emotion or sensation.

Cramer is sparing in his use of direct quotations. He uses the voice of the television commmentator to good effect and members of the family speak as necessary. Many of the direct quotations, in providing contrast, also show irony. One that is particularly concise yet strong appears near the end of the story.

All at once, there was no crowd at all. Just a few people, who seemed not to know where to go.

Three girls in tight blue jeans and heavy makeup walked away. One said: "Let's go watch on TV."

The reader appreciates the irony because the reader knows what the television screen is showing. And it is not what is happening in the streets.

Chapter Four
The Suspect

BACKGROUND

Within 2 hours of an attempted assassination of President Ronald Reagan, a team of reporters and a primary writer at *The Philadelphia Inquirer* began collecting information for a comprehensive story on the man accused of the crime. Approximately 48 hours later, the work of 13 reporters and some wire service reports had been shaped into a narrative by Donald C. Drake, the *Inquirer*'s medical writer. Drake, who spent approximately 8 hours writing the story, used his pre-writing time to organize the reporters' notes so that the narrative he produced would have at the outset a tension to propel the reader through to the story's end. Drake realized that the readers would know how the story ended so he sought to retain their interest by showing what the accused did. The story reproduced here appeared in the first edition. With photographs, it occuppied approximately three full newspaper pages. Drake updated the story for the final edition. The reporters whose work Drake shaped into this story are Tom Belden, Mark Bowden, Larry Eichel, Lucinda Fleeson, Linda Herskowitz, Timothy Lemmer, Rick Nichols, Carol Horner, Arthur Howe, Jane P. Shoemaker, David Zucchino, and correspondent D. W. Nauss.

BIOGRAPHY

Donald C. Drake majored in English literature and government at New York University before dropping out in his junior year to pursue a writing career. "I wanted to be a playwright," Drake says, "but coming from a bohemian Greenwich Village background, I developed an aversion to periodic poverty, so I compromised and became a newspaperman entitled to a weekly paycheck." He worked as copyboy for the *New York Herald-Tribune* and then for five other newspapers and one medical magazine. He established the first science-medical beat at *Newsday* and joined the *Inquirer* in 1966. He is the author of *Medical School*, a book based on an *Inquirer* series that followed a class of students through their 4 years in medical school.

THE STORY

The Suspect

From a lonely childhood to a D.C. Jail

(Thursday, April 2, 1981.
Reprinted with permission
from *The Philadelphia Inquirer*, 1981.)

It was a sunny Sunday afternoon. Washington's cherry blossoms had just begun their annual bloom. Tourists walked past the White House. Two blocks away, at the Park Central—a quiet, small hotel across the street from the headquarters of the Secret Service—a blond young man, unshaven and looking worn out, arrived a little before 1. The young man had just finished an exhausting three-day odyssey by bus across America from California.

He walked through a small lobby and checked in, paying $47 in advance because he had not made a reservation. He went to Room 312, a small, comfortably furnished room that opened onto an inner courtyard.

He carried with him a suitcase, a $47 handgun and a letter describing how he intended to assassinate the President of the United States.

•

Within hours after John W. Hinckley Jr., 25, was arrested and charged in the shooting of President Reagan and three others, a flood of information about this heretofore unknown man was quickily assembled. But it merely whetted the appetite for understanding. It gave no rational explanation for his actions.

A dozen Inquirer reporters went to most of the places known to have shaped the life of John Hinckley since his name became so familiar on Monday. What emerged from those who knew him—and no one seemed to know him intimately—is a portrait of a drifter, a loner, someone who appeared to be preoccupied with unspoken thoughts. He had been taking tranquilizers and was known to be under psychiatric care.

In Lubbock, Texas, where he spent seven years at Texas Technological University but never received a degree, he wasted days on end in a dark room watching a rental television and eating hamburgers from fast-food places. Occasionally he emerged to browse in the books on Nazi Germany at a used bookstore.

In Evergreen, Colo., an affluent suburb of Denver, the recollections are mostly of Hinckley's religiously active millionaire father and of the young man's well-liked brother and sister, John Jr. spent weeks living nearby without his own family knowing it.

In Nashville, Tenn., airport security agents tell how they stopped Hinckley when an X-ray of his luggage showed the silhouettes of three handguns, 50 rounds of ammunition and a pair of handcuffs. Four days later he was in Dallas, buying the gun that would later be used to shoot the President.

And the leader of one group of American neo-Nazis remembers meeting Hinckley—

clad in brown shirt and jackboots—at a Nazi parade in St. Louis and of having determined that Hinckley was somehow off-key, too violent even for them.

Everywhere he went he left hints of a troubled, isolated personality, of a youth alienated from his family and separate from his peers, of an angry man whose only obvious interests were guns, fascism and fast-food hamburgers.

The definitive story of John Warnock Hinckley Jr. may not be known for years, if ever. What is now clear is the account of a twisted life and of the forces that impelled a young man to make a cross-country journey that ended at a perch just outside the Washington Hilton Hotel—where, on a drizzly Monday afternoon, he allegedly fired six shots from a .22-caliber pistol and hit the President.

It starts in Lubbock, Texas.

•

"Oh, boy, here comes Hinky-Dinky," the man in the television rental shop would yell to his partner each morning when he saw John Hinckley Jr. coming down the street, bound for Bill's Lot-A-Burger to buy his breakfast, a half-pound Texas jumbo burger.

He did it every morning about 10. Casually clad, usually in faded jeans and a T-shirt, Hinckley would trudge past the window of the Lubbock rental business, only to walk back a few minutes later with the white paper bag containing the burger under his arm.

They remembered Hinckley at Acco Rentals because they couldn't understand why the young man, a student at Texas Tech, would spend a couple of hundred dollars over an 18-month period renting a succession of cheap black and white television sets, any one of which he could have purchased for $75.

Checking his records the other day, Don Barrett, Acco's owner, determined that Hinckley had come into the shop 51 times to make payments and chat a bit—mostly about the Dallas Cowboys and the Texas Tech Red Raiders, who played in the stadium across the street from Acco and from the nearby apartment building where Hinckley lived. He would stay 10 to 15 minutes and then leave without ever revealing much about himself.

Barrett and his partner began to think that those business transactions were Hinckley's only regular human contact. On one occasion, when Hinckley was uncharacteristically late with a payment, Barrett visited Hinckley's rented room, more as a friendly gesture than a desire to get the money. It was almost completely bare, Barrett recalled.

A film of dust, from the dust storms that plague the West Texas flatland, covered the furniture. No cooking utensils were evident. The blinds were drawn. The only signs of life were a guitar resting on the sofa, the rental television perched on a chair and a table piled high with empty white Lot-A-Burger bags.

He made no more of an impression at Westernair Apartments, where Hinckley lived briefly—from Jan. 5 to May 31, 1979—and paid $175 a month rent.

"I didn't get to know him very well," said Kevin P. Crowley, an engineering student who manages the complex. "I'd see him at the pool. He was polite, quiet . . . He was inward, he didn't talk. The girl next door to him said she didn't even know him.

"He was the kind of guy where, if you walked by him and he knew your face but you didn't say anything, then he wouldn't say anything either."

A few miles away, on the Texas Tech campus, Hinckley left little more of an impression. Otto Nelson, who taught German history, recalled that Hinckley always came to class alone and sat in the back of the room, by himself.

Another thing Nelson remembered: Hinckley had done a rather good book report.

It was on Adolf Hitler's 700-page autobiography, *Mein Kampf*. Nelson had been bemused that summer of 1978 when Hinckley had selected the book for study.

"I can't see much reason for reading *Mein Kampf*," the professor said. "It's so turgid and awful. It's not at all entertaining."

Mein Kampf certainly was not popular reading material in the small Texas Panhandle community or at the particularly conservative university. But Hinckley evidently determined that he had to have his own copy of Hitler's book.

Lonnie Montgomery, owner of Montgomery's Used Books, remembers Hinckley as the young man who, in April 1980, took a particular interest in the 500 World War II volumes that Montgomery had bought from a collector.

"He came in about 12 times," Montgomery recalled. "He never said anything, but he would stand in the back for 30 minutes to an hour, just browsing through the World War II books."

On one of these visits to the store, Hinckley paid $30 for a 10-year-old, two-volume edition of *Mein Kampf*.

Calvin Wynne, a maintenance man at the University Arms Apartments, one of the many residences Hinckley rented in his seven years of sporadic studies at Texas Tech, recalls having a political discussion with Hinckley last year.

They were standing near the apartment's pool, and, Wynne remembered, Hinckley appeared nervous. "He moved around a lot," Wynne said. They discussed the presidential campaign and the various candidates, including Ed Clark, the Libertarian. "He said if he had to make a choice, he would pick Clark," Wynne said, "but as far as he was concerned none of them knew what he was doing."

Hinckley also once told Wynne that he thought that all political leaders should be eliminated. "He just basically had no allegiance to any authoritarian control," Wynne said.

There was more to Hinckley's insular life in Lubbock than just hamburgers and Hitler. There were guns. An official of the office of the federal Bureau of Alcohol, Tobacco and Firearms confirmed yesterday that records showed that Hinckley had purchased at least six handguns over 18 months from various Lubbock pawnshops.

Should that have raised a warning signal somewhere?

"Naw," the official said. "We have people that buy a hundred or two hundred a year around here."

Rolf Gordhamer, who directs psychological testing and counseling at Texas Tech, said it was quite common for students to carry weapons at the college.

"Seriously," he said, "this is frontierland. People do have guns. Their grandparents were pioneers. There are a lot of small towns and isolation, and change comes very slowly. People shoot rattlesnakes and coyotes and," he paused to laugh, "trespassers."

As for Hinckley, until last Monday, Gordhamer had never heard of him either. For all of the young man's psychiatric problems, there is no indication, Gordhamer said, that he sought help from Gordhamer's office. "We simply don't have any record of him."

One person who did keep a record of dealings with Hinckley in Lubbock was Wayne Whitson, the owner of the Snidely Whiplash Pawn Shop. It was there last September that Hinckley bought two pearl-handled .22-caliber pistols for $200 apiece.

This week, Whitson, a swarthy man with a gold Texas-shaped medallion dangling from his neck, marveled at the skill of the man accused of firing six shots and wounding four people:

"When you hit with four out of six shots in 2½ seconds, that's pretty good," Whitson said. "I wouldn't believe that he could pull the trigger that fast."

•

Last Novmember, one of the biggest majorities that Ronald Reagan received in his bid for the presidency was rolled up in a well-to-do area outside Dallas called Park Cities. It was there that John Warnock Hinckley Sr. became a millionaire oilman, a devout Christian who attends a weekly Bible-reading club and a devotee of the politics of Ronald Reagan. And it was there that John Warnock Hinckley Jr. was raised.

The man charged in the shooting of President Reagan was born in Ardmore, Okla., on May 29, 1955, the last of three children of John and Joanne Hinckley. The family moved to Dallas in 1966; eight years later they moved again, to the affluent "paradise community" of Evergreen, Colo., outside Denver. But John Jr. had little association with the family's comfortable life there. He was mostly raised in the suburbs of Dallas, where even as a child, he was quiet, withdrawn.

"He and other children from the neighborhood used to come over for cookies and milk," said Toni Johnson, a neighbor who knew Hinckley in the late 1950s and early 1960s. "He would never talk, I don't remember him every saying anything, I asked the other kids, my own, if there was something wrong with him. He was always clean and neat, but it always seemed strange to me that a child of that age, I guess he was about 6 then, never talked."

After graduating from Highland Park High School in 1974, Hinckley enrolled at Texas Tech as a business administration major. He attended school sporadically, subsequently changing his major to English. Some people remembered him as wanting to become a playwright. His grades in college hovered between B and C averages.

As he drifted in and out of the campus, up and down the West, he tried occasionally to find steady work. He applied unsuccessfully late last year for a job with the two Denver newspapers, the Post and the Rocky Mountain News. His job applications cited experience as a salesman in Hollywood, a bartender in Denver and a bookkeeper in Dallas.

But he always seemed to return to the arid, inhospitable land of Lubbock, where summer temperatures reached 105 or more and the residents advise not to laugh during windstorms lest you choke to death on dust.

John's older brother, Scott, and sister, Diane, seemed to have been more successful than he was, at least according to the standards expressed by the family's lifestyle. Friends said Diane, three years older than John, was an exuberant cheerleader in high school, a memorably alert young woman who overshadowed her younger brother. The mother of two, she and her husband now live in Dallas. Scott, about six years older than John, is vice president of the family's $5 million oil business, the Denver-based Vanderbilt Energy Corp.

The family is well off and well positioned socially. Just last Tuesday, Scott Hinckley was to have been a dinner guest at the Denver home of Neil Bush, whose father is vice president of the United States. The dinner party was cancelled after the arrest of Scott's brother the previous day.

John Hinckley Jr. has recently been under psychiatric care and was taking Valium, a commonly prescribed tranquilizer, his family said this week.

•

Dr. John Nichols, a Pennsylvania State University journalism professor and author of the book *The Mind of the Assassins*,[1] said: "Mental illness, psychosis, insanity or whatever such term one wishes to use, is one of the essential ingredients of assassinations, American style. Without it there would have been no assassinations."

Writing in the magazine Psychology Today, Dr. Irving D. Harris, a Chicago psychiatrist said: "America's assassins have almost always been younger children in their families, and in most cases they have had older brothers. . . . Their one-down family position predisposes them to rebel against authority and tradition, to resent their unequal status and to wish to gain status by competing with the successful rival or by weakening the power of authorities. . . . If these feelings find no constructive outlet, then a shortcut to fame may seem reasonable."

•

Evergreen, Colo., is a mountain town of striking beauty. Around nearly every bend in its roads, snow-capped gray rock cliffs loosely cloaked with spruce and fir jut over clear blue lakes.

Hiwan, the site of the Hinckley family home, is a sprawling, 1,068-acre development built to capitalize on this Colorado grandeur. Thirty-five mountainous miles west of Denver, it is too remote for spur-of-the-moment visits to the city, but it is successful because of its beauty.

Only 140 of Hiwan's 600 capacious lots remain unbuilt and uninhabited. Its homes— towering two- and three-story wood and stone frame structures that sell for between $150,000 and $500,000—are on a scale as grand as the surroundings. A rolling green country club is its centerpiece, its aesthetic and social center. Hiwan's homes are luxuriously furnished, with high ceilings and wide sunny rooms. Inside and out, it is a rich community.

"That's why we couldn't believe it when we heard this guy was from Evergreen," said Marge MacDonald, who runs a small bookshop in the fashionable shopping area about five miles from the Hinckley home. "I mean, this place is so idyllic it's like a fantasy community, it's so beautiful. And Hiwan! Hiwan is the top of the line!"

John Hinckley's family fit in. They are known to nearly every other family in the development, even those living several miles away. Praise for the family is instant and insistent. After the news of Hinckley's arrest was broadcast, neighbors closed ranks behind the family. To a person, they refused to comment in detail. They would say only that the Hinckleys were "wonderful" or "charming," and the elder Hinckley was praised as a kind and friendly man active in community affairs, well known and well liked.

Here, as elsewhere, no one seemed to know his second son, John Jr.

"They are dear, dear people," said Mrs. Thomas Williams, a well-dressed, grayhaired woman who lives about a mile north. "I know them personally from the club, and I feel so sorry for them. I have been wanting to go visit them, but with all the

---

[1]The actual author of the book is the late Dr. Donald W. Hastings, a psychiatrist. Dr. Nichols represents Dr. Hastings' estate as an agent for the still unpublished manuscript. This fact error, while regretable, does not detract from the technique.

reporters and cameras there I've been afraid. I know their older boy and their girl, but I don't believe I was ever introduced to young John. He was never around, and the family never spoke of him to me. It's such a shock.''

When the Hinckleys moved to Hiwan in 1974, John Jr. was one year out of high school. It was a family move that apparently never really included the youngest child.

Indeed, as time went by, his parents were living at the center of a comfortable, affluent community, widely known and admired. But young Hinckley took to staying alone in a motel room less than 20 miles away, known to almost no one. Investigators trying to find some trace of Hinckley's existence in Evergreen have found only a scattering of job applications, apparently filled in with much false information, all of them leading nowhere.

At bars, record shops and bookstores where the few young people of Evergreen congregate, no one knew John Hinckley. His anonymity is unusual in such a small, relatively isolated town.

''He mustn't have spent much time here or we would know him,'' said a waitress at Dos Amigos, a small tavern in Evergreen. ''Everybody knows everybody in Evergreen.''

One man remembered John Hinckley Jr., but only vaguely. Jesse Hahn, a tall and lean security guard employed by a private agency, said he recalled Hinckley's name and face when he saw television reports on the shooting Monday. Hahn said that he did not know the young man well but that he remembered dealing with him about a year ago when Hahn was working as a salesman at a local sporting goods store. Hahn said he remembered distinctly what he sold Hinckley. It was a handgun.

•

On March 11, 1978, Michael C. Allen was preparing for the celebration of the 60th anniversary of the birth of the late George Lincoln Rockwell, founder of the American Nazi Party. Allen, then leader of the St. Louis section of the National Socialist Party, greeted 100 or so neo-Nazis and supporters gathering in party headquarters prior to a motorcade. A young sandy-haired man came up to him to talk.

Allen was surprised, he remembers, that he didn't recognize someone clad in complete Nazi, stormtrooper regalia—brown work shirt, belt ensemble, swastika armband, military trousers and jackboots. The young man said he was John Hinckley and he wanted to join the party.

''Mr. Hinckley, upon first impression, seemed to be a likable enough fellow,'' Allen recalled. ''Aside from being a Nazi, he did not seem too out of the ordinary.''

Harold Covington, a Raleigh, N.C., man who was also a leader of the neo-Nazi group, remembers having met but taken little note of Hinckley at the St. Louis rally. But Hinckley evidently remembered Covington, who said this week that he received 10 or 12 letters from the young man after Hinckley returned to Texas.

''He wrote that he was interested in what he could do for the party,'' Covington said. ''But it quickly became apparent to me that he felt we were not sufficiently militant for him. We developed quite a difference of opinion on the dynamics of revolution. He was interested in violence, in shooting people. He was quite radical in his thinking.''

Covington insists that he told Hinckley ''over and over'' that the organization was not interested in violence.

Allen said he too came to distrust Hinckley. ''Rallies and demonstrations were not enough,'' Allen said of Hinckley this week. "He said he believed violence and bloodshed was the answer. He advocated illegal acts, and we believe in acting within the law. We don't want his kind in our organization.''

All the same, Hinckley had joined the party. According to Covington, there was no unit in Lubbock, but Hinckley seemed to have enlisted in a chapter in Pasadena, a suburb of Houston. In 1979, the party's leader in Texas, Michael Breda, filed a report on Hinckley to Frank Collin, the party's national commander in Chicago. Recalling the report, Allen said it described Hinckley as "violent, irrational and advocated to terrorism.''

Allen continued:

"The report said local [Pasadena, Texas] members had been unable to persuade Mr. Hinckley to refrain from his violent threats and to conform with party philosophy. Because of his radical beliefs, it was recommended that his membership not be renewed.'' The membership was not renewed.

•

Swinging a large gray suitcase, a young man came running down the south concourse of the Nashville Metropolitan Airport, late, apparently, for a departing plane.

Reaching a security checkpoint and the X-ray machine for hand luggage, the man yelled to Evelyn Braun, a sergeant for Wackenhut Security Corp., who was on duty at the checkpoint.

"I'm running late,'' he said, as she remembers the incident on Oct. 9. "You gotta put that through,'' he added, referring to the luggage that he was carrying.

The man was John Hinckley, and Mrs. Braun thought that he looked suspicious because, she later explained, he appeared more nervous than rushed.

Mrs. Braun instead indicated to an associate, Laura Farmer, to check the bag very carefully.

While Mrs. Farmer waited for the image to appear on the machine, Mrs. Braun explained to Hinckley that the bag had to be checked, that it could not be taken on the plane as hand luggage. It was the rule, she said.

As shadowy outlines of the contents of Hinckley's bag emerged on the screen, Mrs. Farmer found what she was looking for. A signal was flashed to security officer John A. Lynch, standing about 15 feet away. He walked over to the two women and the nervous young man.

What they found

The suitcase was opened and there, lying amid clothes that seemed to have been hastily thrown into the suitcase, were two .22-caliber revolvers, a .38-caliber revolver, 50 .22-caliber Winchester cartridges and a set of handcuffs.

According to Mrs. Braun, Hinckley tried to explain that he was going to try to sell the weapons, that he was late for his plane, that he had to go. But Lynch would not let him go and instead began to recite his legal rights to Hinckley. Lynch noticed that Hinckley's hands were shaking.

As Hinckley was taken off to court, the FBI—as is customary—was notified of the arrest.

"Usually when we notify the FBI, they meet us downtown and talk to the suspect, but this day they all apparently were tied up with the President's visit to Nashville,'' Lynch said.

As the arrest took place, President Jimmy Carter was addressing a town meeting five miles away, at the Grand Ole Opry House. A few hours later, he was scheduled to pass through the Nashville airport. Officials in Nashville said no one drew a connection between Carter's presence and Hinckley's possession of the handguns because Hinckley was leaving the airport, rather than arriving

The Secret Service was not notified of the arrest. Hinckley's name was not put on the computerized list of potential assassins maintained at Secret Service offices in Washington.

Hinckley was brought to the Nashville police headquarters and jail, where he was taken before General Sessions Judge William E. Higgins. Standing before the judge in a tiny room at the back of police headquarters, Hinckley heard Higgins tell him that the maximum fine for carrying a weapon was $50 and that the court charges were $12.50. The judge said that Hinckley could come back in a couple of weeks and stand trial or that he could pay the $62.50 then.

Hinckley had barely enough money, but he paid the fine and court charge and was driven back to the airport—leaving behind the guns, ammunition and handcuffs.

Four days later Hinckley was in Dallas, buying two more guns. One of them would be identified as the gun used to shoot Ronald Reagan.

•

The east end of downtown Dallas is a deteriorating section in the shadows of the booming business district's new skyscrapers. Along East Elm Street, not far from Dallas police headquarters, there is a string of pawn shops, beer bars and bail bond offices.

On Oct. 13, 1980, John Hinckley made his way to 2018 E. Elm and a shop whose front was adorned with a sign declaring: "Rocky's Pawn Shop, Police Equipment, Sam Browne Outfits, Guns."

Inquiring about handguns, Hinckley was shown a variety of weapons by David Goldstein, son of the owner, who is known as Rocky. Hinckley bought two R.G.-14 .22-caliber revolvers with short blue steel barrels, guns commonly known as "Saturday night specials." Because of their poor quality, they are not considered suitable for use by sportsmen.

Following standard procedure, David Goldstein asked Hinckley for identification. The young man presented a driver's license with a Lubbock address. Listing his birthplace as Ardmore, Okla., and signing a document that said he did not have a police record, Hinckley paid $47.95 for each of the two guns and left.

•

Just two weeks ago, two men from World Vision Inc., a California-based Christian organization, went to the Denver office of John W. Hinckley Sr. to discuss the group's work in Africa.

Hinckley was a natural contact for the Christian activists. A committed Christian and philanthropist, he once had flown to Biafra to help coordinate relief efforts there. He was planning a trip to Guatemala in connection with an anti-hunger project he intended to support there.

Nor were Hinckley's charitable efforts directed only to the unfortunate in other nations. In 1976 and 1977, Hinckley and two other oil executives helped to underwrite the operation of a small Christian mission in a blighted Denver neighborhood of pawn shops, warehouses and cheap bars near the railroad yards. On Sunday Hinckley would go to the mission to preach to the alcoholics and bums.

When problems developed in the operation of that street mission, Hinckley and the others decided to channel their money into the Denver Rescue Mission, an older and more established Christian mission in the same tawdry neighborhood.

When the World Vision representatives arrived for the meeting, Hinckley began the session, as was his custom, with a brief devotion. Head bowed, the oilman said he was anxious about his son, whom he described as "wayward" and "lacking any direction in his life." He asked that the visitors pray for his son, John. Jr.

•

John Hinckley checked into the Golden Hours Motel the morning of March 8, 1981. It was one of dozens of cheap motels along West Colfax Avenue in Lakewood, a bedroom community to the west of Denver.

The motel had a slanted roof and coral figerglass panels. In front was a chrome and yellow neon sign. One of five blue stars attached by wire to the sign was loose and jiggled in the wind.

Hinckley was registered by the motel owner, Bok Soon Lee, an Oriental with one gold tooth. She could barely speak English, but it didn't matter because Hinckley didn't talk much. She assigned him to Room 30, on the second floor. Hinckley reached the room by walking through the parking lot, going up a staircase and passing through an outdoor corridor of bumpy, warped rubber mats.

Hinckley stayed in this motel, a short drive from his parents' opulent home, for 16 solitary days. Every morning he would be out by 9 and back by 11 or 11:30. For the rest of the day he'd be in and out. He told people in the motel that he worked at a record shop and even offered to get them records, though he apparently had no job.

Frequently he would dodge the traffic to cross a six-lane highway in front of the motel to go to a McDonald's. Some days he would eat all three meals there.

He struck up an acquaintance of sorts with Ginger Acourt, a motel maid who lived in an adjoining room with her three children. Ms. Aucort, a big woman with square hands and square face, said Hinckley talked only about music and Dallas, and never mentioned the family living only 20 miles away in affluent Evergreen.

"He seemed lonely, but not depressed," remembered Stacey Aucort, 16. "He was shy. You would have to speak to him before he'd talk to you and you would have to keep saying something or he'd just keep walking."

Though Hinckley led a quiet existence here, his behavior appeared odd to Lakewood patrolman Chris Warsham, who on March 18 noticed Hinckley staring at Warsham's patrol car while crossing the highway bound for McDonald's. Warsham was sufficiently suspicious to turn his patrol car around and watch Hinckley disappear into the fast-food restaurant. He waited 20 minutes until he saw Hinckley slip out the back door of the restaurant, headed back for the motel.

Inquiring about Hinckley at the motel, the beefy cop, who was 29 with more than seven years on the force, went to Room 30 and knocked on the door. Getting no response, he suddenly became nervous about his own safety and drew his handgun. Hinckley apparently was not in the room, and Warsham holstered his weapon. An hour later the policeman caught up with Hinckley in the motel parking lot.

Warsham remembers Hinckley keeping his face averted as he answered the patrolman's questions with curt "Yessirs" and "Nossirs." The policeman had no reason to detain the young man, so he let him go.

Hinckley never told anyone at the motel what he did when he left on his afternoon excursions, but on several occasions, he went to the Denver Rescue Mission, the agency that was supported by his father.

A clean, neat young man in a sea of unshaven, unkempt bums with bugs in their clothes and cheap wine in their bellies, Hinckley was conspicuous. But the Rev. Le-Roy Bradrick, a preacher for the last 30 of his 64 years, did not treat Hinckley any differently from the derelicts. He learned long ago, he said, that it doesn't matter how they look on the outside; inside they are all the same—and their souls have to be saved.

So dinner in the rescue mission did not come without a price: listening to an hour's worth of gospel music and preaching. On the nights he was there, Hinckley shuffled in with the others—about a hundred men showed up on an average night—when the doors opened at 6:30. They filed into the chapel, settled themselves on the folding metal chairs and, each time, heard a plea to let Jesus take hold of their lives.

On his fourth or perhaps fifth visit, Hinckley showed up in an olive green jacket with a backpack slung on his shoulders and an electric guitar under his arm. He was interested in more than a meal this night; he needed money.

He went up to one man who had given up life in the gutter for God three years earlier and now helps to run the mission. Asking to speak to the man privately, Hinckley got him to step outside, where, under an orange neon sign declaring that "Jesus Saves," Hinckley offered to sell his electric guitar.

The older man rejected the offer. No, he said, money does not solve problems. Hinckley never returned.

Hinckley subsequently walked into G.I. Joe's Pawn Shop, in Denver's skid row a few doors from the Salvation Army.

He carried with him his electric guitar and a manual typewriter. Something bothered the associate manager, Jonathan Morris.

"You size up people real quick in this business," Morris recalled, "and I got the feeling, the way he talked—he was nervous—that things were not normal with this man. I thought he was a little off. He looked a little down on his luck."

At first the pawn-shop operator didn't want to buy the merchandise. The guitar had a Social Security number etched on its back, raising to Morris the possibility it had been stolen. Morris checked with police and, assured that it was not listed as stolen, gave Hinckley $50.

Before Hinckley left the shop, he asked directions to the bus station. Hinckley mumbled something that Morris is not sure about now because someone else came into the shop, but he thinks that Hinckley said something about taking the bus to Washington.

•

On March 25, John W. Hinckley Jr. got into his 1973 Plymouth Volare at the Golden Rest Motel and headed away. He abandoned the car near his parents' home and made his way to Stapleton International Airport, where he boarded a Western Airlines flight at 11:45 a.m., taking the Boeing 737 jet to Salt Lake City, Utah. It arrived at 12:40 p.m. He hurried to catch a 1:10 p.m. connecting flight to Los Angeles International Airport.

Hinckley paid cash—$89—for the roundabout trip to Los Angeles. It was an instance of frugality. By taking the connection instead of a direct Denver-to-Los Angeles flight, he qualified for a Western Airlines discount from the normal $194 coach fare.

The plane touched down in Los Angeles at 2:08 p.m. Hinckley took a bus from the airport to Hollywood, where he registered at the Sunset Palms Motel on a section of Sunset Boulevard known as the Sunset Strip. The cheap motel is frequented by prostitutes, junkies and transients.

Authorities in Los Angeles say they have no idea why Hinckley went there. All they know is that he stayed one night in the motel, then left.

(In 1976, he had lived in roughly the same neighborhood for three months beginning in April. His home was a Howard's Weekly Apartments on El Centro Avenue in Hollywood, where he rented a one-room studio apartment on the third floor. When he registered, he gave a hotel in Lubbock as his previous address.)

In any case, last Thursday, March 26, 1981, Hinckley boarded a bus in Los Angeles and headed east on a three-day trip that brought him to the Greyhound bus terminal in Washington on Sunday, March 29.

Linda Ross, 30, a waitress at the Burger King in the Washington bus station, waited on Hinckley at lunchtime that day.

"I have a bad habit of watching people's eyes," she said. "His eyes were darting all over the place. Sometimes you can tell the way people feel just by the way they walk and talk. He seemed very upset, like he had a lot on his mind. He had a real bad odor."

It is not known why Hinckley chose to stay in the Park Central or how he got there from the bus station. It is not far away. Even for someone carrying a suitcase, it was less than a 30-minute walk. And the hotel was advertised in the Yellow Pages as being near the White House.

Hinckley arrived at the Park Central at 1 p.m., walked across the lobby and checked in. He got the key for Room 312.

•

Hinckley arrived in Washington unremarked. In a little more than 24 hours his name would be known throughout the world. His picture would be on television and the front pages of newspapers everywhere as the man accused of shooting the President.

In a little more than 24 hours this man would find himself shackled to a chain soldered to the metal desk in the headquarters of the Metropolitan Police where local authorities and the FBI discussed whether the city or the federal government would have jurisdiction in the shooting case. Word would come out that the President himself had been shot, and the FBI would take the case.

Red wax would seal the door of Room 312 of the Park Central—even the keyhole would be covered—and a sign would proclaim that the room had been shut off because it contained important evidence.

•

John Hinckley awoke early the morning of March 30. He was gone from his hotel room by the time Sue, a third-floor maid who had emigrated the the United States from West Africa, got there to clean the room. He probably was eating breakfast. The people at the nearby Kay's Sandwich Shoppe have a vague recollection that he ate there.

At the same time, two blocks away in the White House, President Reagan was having breakfast with leaders of his administration prior to delivering a speech to a labor conference at the Washington Hilton Hotel.

Sue returned to Room 312 about 1:15 p.m. and knocked on the door, thinking that the guest had checked out because he had registered only for one night. But a voice answered her knock.

"What?" a young man with blond hair said when she stuck her head in. He was standing near the bathroom. She said she had come to see if there were enough towels in the room.

"I need a pillowslip," he said, staying where he was, drinking from a can of soda. He spoke to her in a calm, unexcited manner, but did not move away from the bathroom door while she busied herself with her chores. She asked if he would be staying. He said:

"I'm spending the night."

Less than an hour later, Hinckley was standing at a side entrance of the Washington Hilton, near a sharply curving, eight-foot-high stone wall. There was a crowd of people, many of them photographers and reporters, waiting for the President to leave the meeting of the AFL-CIO.

Among the bystanders was Adrian Seay, 19. "It's rainy, but it's too nice to be out here," Hinckley said to Seay. It seemed a strange comment. It didn't make any sense. Seay said it made him uneasy, so he backed away. "I'll see you," Seay said.

"You won't see me anymore," Hinckley replied.

Inside the hotel, President Reagan was just finishing his speech. Polite applause followed and Reagan walked from the International Ballroom of the hotel up one flight to a terrace-level doorway known as the presidential entrance.

Hinckley hugged the rain-spattered stone wall outside, and thus his view of the door where the President would soon emerge was blocked. All he could see was the glass-and-stone office building across the street that looms a block long.

Through the building's windows, he could see the secretaries working at their desks under the fluorescent lights and a mish-mash of signs on the building's ground floor advertising doughnuts, bread and bagels, coffee shoppe, patent medicines, cosmetics, souvenirs, greeting cards, photo needs.

The President emerged from the brown steel doors of the hotel, surrounded by police, Secret Service agents and his aides. He was smiling and waved to the crowds, first with his right hand and then with his left.

Hinckley stepped out away from the wall and aimed his gun. As he stepped out, the hotel's American flag came into his view.

He fired.

DISCUSSION

Like good writers of fiction, Drake opens his story simply, immediately establishing his reporting voice. Andre Fontaine (1974), the author of a textbook on writing in-depth newspaper articles, said:

> Narrative is one of the things a good interpretive writer borrows from fiction writers. It is telling a story, building suspense, putting your characters (and the reader) into a situation, then taking them through it, complete with emotional involvements, to a resolution. It's not changing facts, but arranging them. It is plotting. (p. 280)

Drake did plot this story. He envisioned it as a series of scenes (discussed shortly), which he outlined before he sat down to write. "I knew that the first scene would begin in the hotel and the last scene would end outside the hotel with Hinckley firing his gun,'' Drake says.

Drake wanted to develop tension at the beginning of the story so it would propel the reader through the story. ''When stories are many thousand words long, the newspaper reader, I believe, will lose interest unless there are certain seductive qualities built into the story to make him want to find answers to questions that have developed in his mind,'' Drake says. Drake opened with the hotel because he figured that even though the readers knew what Hinckley was going to do, they would stay with the story to see how he did it.

Drake says:

> When you stop to think about it so many suspense movies start with the main character about to do something and then the camera switches to another scene. All the time the camera is exploring these other areas, the moviegoer is waiting for the camera to return to the scene that opened the movie and continue with the action that was so suspenseful at that moment.

Drake also uses foreshadowing, a literary technique that provides hints of what is to come. He cites as an example something he read in a playwriting book.

> You're writing a scene in which a woman, preparing for bed, is knifed to death by an intruder. There are two ways to tell this scene. You can open it with the woman sitting in front of her mirror, combing her hair, and suddenly have the intruder burst out of the closet and stab her. This would be an exciting moment, but unfortunately, it would be only a moment. Another way to tell the same scene is to do what I try to do in my stories. Open the scene with the intruder entering the closet and closing it after him. Then have the woman come on stage, sit in front of the mirror and start combing her hair. From the moment she walks onto the stage until the intruder bursts from the closet, the audience is very tense because it knows what will certainly happen.

Drake organized his story into 14 scenes. Some of them foreshadow events, some are flashbacks, some are expositions. A summary of the scenes looks like this:

Scene 1—The opening scene foreshadows events. The reader is told that the main character intends to assassinate the president of the United States. In scene 13, after several flashbacks and/or expositions, Drake ties the story back to this scene.

Scene 2—This scene outlines the story to come. In effect, it is the story's *raison d'etre*. Drake uses it to say what the story is about.

Scene 3—This is the story's first flashback. In this scene, Drake takes the reader to Hinckley's student days at Texas Tech. In a later flashback, Drake will go farther back in time.

In this particular scene Drake also subtly foreshadows Hinckley's eventual membership in the American Nazi Party. The foreshadowing occurs through the reference to *Mein Kampf*, although Drake does not suggest that anything will come of this. The reader must learn things in their proper sequence.

Scene 4—This is the second flashback of the story. This one goes back into Hinckley's childhood.

Scene 5—This is not really a scene but a brief exposition on assassins. This does help establish irony.

Scene 6—Drake is now establishing what the current Hinckley Sr. homestead in Evergreen, Colorado, is like. In scene 11, Hinckley will live nearby, in the month before he attempts to assassinate the president.

Scene 7—This scene tells of Hinckley's short-lived affiliation with the American Nazi Party. For the reader who recalls the reference to *Mein Kampf* in scene 3, scene 7 provides additional insight into Hinckley's character.

Scene 8—The opening scene mentioned a $47 handgun. But that was not the only gun Hinckley owned. He owned other guns, and he had at least two contacts with the law. In this scene, Hinckley is arrested and the weapons confiscated. The reader is relieved.

Scene 9—Hinckley buys more weapons. The relief of scene 8 is replaced by tension and anxiety.

Scene 10—Hinckley's father is introduced here and Drake uses the scene to establish more irony (discussed shortly). He also mentions the Christian mission, which will appear again in a different context in the next scene.

Scene 11—All of the time, Drake has been moving the story forward by introducing the reader to Hinckley's past and then moving the story forward to report his current behavior. Thanks to flashbacks, the reader has background on how Hinckley behaves.

Again, a brush with the law makes the reader realize this man came close at least twice to never reaching Washington, DC, and shooting the president. Tension mounts.

Scene 12—Drake tells more about how Hinckley's behavior by showing the circuitous route he took to Washington. The scenes are getting shorter as the tension heightens.

Scene 13—Another short scene. Hinckley arrives in Washington and Drake ties the story back to scene 1.

Scene 14—The deed is done. The tension released. The story ends.

Because of his detached narrative approach to this story, Drake is able to point out ironies. These ironies are not obvious to the characters in the story. Relatively early in the story, Drake reveals irony by showing that Hinckley is the youngest child and then quoting a psychiatrist who says: ''America's assassins have almost always been younger children in their families, and in most cases they have had older brothers.'' Later, Drake relates a scene in which Hinckley's father asks some members of a Christian organization to pray for his son. In a standard journalistic approach, Hinckley's sibling status may have been explained through a psychiatrist's interpretation, but it is unlikely that his father's request for prayers would have been published. Drake, as the narrator, can report everything.

Another aspect of Drake's story that deserves discussion is his use of chronology, which helps emphasize a person's character development. Without detailing each instance, it is still rather easy to see how Drake provides insight into Hinckley's character. He is able to do that because he has plotted his story on a chronological basis with scenes rather than a cause–effect or motive basis, both of which were not known at the time.

A well-plotted story needs tension and resolution. And in fact, Drake rewrote the early part of his story to heighten the drama and to focus the beginning better. He did not have the time or energy to rewrite any more. Rewriting, although virtuous for any writer, is not typical in daily journalism where deadlines are imperative. Nevertheless, as other literary journalists attest, rewriting is critical to producing the desired result.

The final element of Drake's story to be analyzed is the final element—the ending. Typically, newspaper stories just stop. Or as Fontaine (1974) put it, ''Traditional news stories went out with a whimper, but creative journalism demands that stories end with a bang—or at least a snap'' (p. 162). At the *Inquirer*, there was a discussion about changing Drake's ending. ''I had intended,'' he says, ''to end the story with an epilogue stating what happened to Hinckley after he fired the gun. The intention was to break from the narrative flow and state it in expository form.'' The editor for the story wanted the information within the story, but toward the end. Drake considered that cumbersome and he and the editor worked out a compromise ''so that the tension of the final part of the story would not be disturbed.'' Another virtue of the ending is that it stays with the reader even after the reader turns the page. So effective are the final two words that the reader may even shudder or duck after reading them. It is the kind of an ending one expects in a good novel, the kind readers can carry with them after closing the book. It also shows an important element of literary feature writing—the story ending with purpose and by design and not because the writer ran out of information.

Chapter Five
A Job Where
'Nobody Complains'

BACKGROUND

When Paul Shinoff, the labor writer at the San Francisco *Examiner*, proposed a series of stories on "so-called common everyday jobs," he did not expect that one of the series would be about gravediggers. He had first wanted to write about an embalmer and then professional pallbearers, but rejected both for various reasons. He settled on gravediggers, a job type not that common because, as Shinoff found out, many graves are dug with backhoes. He finally found the subjects of this story at an old church cemetery. The cemetery was perfect because, Shinoff says, "I was looking for Irish diggers; they are great colorful talkers. I worked as a member of a predominately Irish Carpenters' Union here for eight years, and that lesson was not lost on me." Other job types in the series called "Punchin In" were a fry cook, supermarket checker, locomotive engineer, telephone operator, bartender, and bridge tolltaker.

BIOGRAPHY

Paul Shinoff studied political science and anthropology at California State University at Northridge, but never received a degree. During and after college, he worked in the garment industry and at a supermarket, as a janitor, lifeguard, seaman in the merchant marine, construction worker, field researcher with aborigines in Australia, cameraman, filmmaker, and longshoreman before becoming an apprentice carpenter in 1970. He made journeyman in 1973 and quit carpentry in 1976 to become a free-lance magazine writer, editor of a labor newspaper, correspondent for the

Washington Post, and ultimately the labor writer for the *Examiner*. He subsequently became an editorial writer for the *Examiner*. He has also served as a lecturer in journalism at San Francisco State University.

THE STORY

A job where 'nobody complains'

(Sunday, September 27, 1981.
© 1981 San Francisco *Examiner*)

Each trade has its own special tricks. A carpenter doesn't just hammer a nail; a waitress doesn't just carry plates. In this occasional series, Examiner Labor Writer Paul Shinoff takes a look at the special tricks that go into seemingly routine jobs, and the men and women who perform them.

By Paul Shinoff
Examiner Staff Writer

The early-morning sun had barely cleared the top of the San Bruno mountains as John Fitzpatrick and Maurice Hickey trudged across the wet, well-manicured lawn of Holy Cross Cemetery, carrying shovels and spades.

Fitzpatrick paused, took a folded yellow slip of paper from the pocket of his faded blue overalls and glanced at the name on the marble headstone.

Planting a heavy rubber boot hard in front of the unadorned monument marked ''Rogerson,'' Fitzpatrick walked off 3½ steps to the side, marked the spot with the corner of a spade, turned and took seven more steps and marked the point again.

He and Hickey drew their spades across the plot, cutting the thick sod into 18 squares, as neatly as a parent dividing a birthday cake.

Working side by side, Fitzpatrick and Hickey then thrust their flat spades under the sod squares, lifting them off like pancakes from a grill.

Each used his personal tool, the blade sharpened on a grinder and then hand-filed to a knife-edge. ''The day I came they gave me a spade, shovel and pick, then sent me out to dig an eight-foot grave,'' said Fitzpatrick.

He is 68 years old and Hickey 69, older than many they labor to put underground. As with all but a handful of the 32 employees at the Colma cemetery, they are foreign-born—''good, sturdy peasant stock'' to quote a San Francisco priest.

Both are heavily muscled. Fitzpatrick is tall and ruddy, with thick white hair. Hickey is a head shorter and deeply tanned; and his dark hair has streaks of sun-bleached blond.

Side by side they work easily, hardly breaking into a sweat. Both start well bundled, tossing layers of sweaters and sweatshirts aside as the sun gets higher and the ground harder.

Neither man has suffered from muscle aches or has ever known the pain of a bad back. Hickey often swims at Aquatic Park, and lifts weights in his basement. He has never called in sick in 30 years.

''There is peace out here and no one complains,'' said Fitzpatrick with a twinkle, gazing across the rows of tombstones.

''In the morning, before people come around, you can listen to the bird songs, the animals come down and you whistle to them, the jack rabbits and the possums and raccoons.''

Neither man is considering retirement. ''What is an old man going to do when he quits work?'' asked Hickey.

''Lie around,'' answered Fitzpatrick with a grunt and a laugh.

They dug steadily for two hours.

★ ★ ★

The term ''grave digger'' is a misnomer—most such work is done by an operator of a $20,000 backhoe tractor, a task that takes no more than a half hour. Hand digging is necessary only in the older sections of cemeteries where machines cannot squeeze through a maze of tombstones.

Holy Cross has 12 to 15 burials a day, but averages no more than two hand-dug graves a week. On days when there is no grave digging to do, Fitzpatrick and Hickey act as pallbearers and groundskeepers.

Neither Fitzpatrick nor Hickey knew anything but the name of the person whose grave they were digging on this recent day.

It was different in rural Ireland, where as a boy Fitzpatrick dug graves as a service for friends and neighbors. There it was a necessary task, not a job.

''Tis one of the corporal works of mercy to bury the dead,'' he explained in a rich country brogue. ''And to visit the sick, feed the hungry—and of course, give a drink to the thirsty.''

Emigrating from Cornafean, County Cavan, in 1955 with his wife, Olive, and baby, Fitzpatrick worked first as a metal polisher, at which he earned $12 a day, and came to Holy Cross because it paid $4 more. The members of the Cemetery Workers Union now earn $84 a day.

The work has traditionally attracted the foreign born. ''In years gone by it was considered degrading,'' explained Hickey. ''But I never thought that—it was a job that had to be done.''

Hickey, who was born in County Waterford, Ireland, came here in 1952 after spending World War II in London, working in bombed-out rubble to bring out the living and the dead.

''Most of these men have known violence and death. They know what it means to suffer and came looking for a better life,'' explained the Rev. Mark Marks, associate pastor of St. Paul's Church in San Francisco, who worked six summers at Holy Cross.

On the average, employees stay at Holy Cross at least 30 years and rarely retire before they're 70. The cemetery offers them free services, so many are buried there. That is the only time that work stops for a funeral. The mourners come in dirt-stained overalls.

''Well over 30 men I worked with are dead and gone,'' said Fitzpatrick. ''Honest men who earned their bread by the sweat of their brow. But I don't think much about the dying. When you prepare for it, you've got nothing to worry about.''

Hickey has purchased a plot next to that of his brother-in-law. He often tends the grounds in that section.

''There are times, just walking from one section to another, when I will pass the grave of a friend, someone I worked with, and say a little prayer.''

Both wish to be buried in simple wooden coffins. ''Even the expensive metal ones do not last,'' said Fitzpatrick. ''We see them come out in pieces.

''The skull is the last thing that decays. We have dug up many of them. I lift them out with my hand, dig a little hole and cover it up again. Yes, the skull is the last, and the shin bone.

''All I want is two feet of dirt over a box. Enough to grow a lawn.''

★ ★ ★

Holy Cross is the oldest of the 18 cemeteries in Colma, San Francisco's suburb of the dead. Burials here began on June 6, 1887. There's a question of who was the first. Fitzpatrick says it was a man named Timothy Buckley. Cemetery records, however, reflect two entries on that first day: Buckley and Bridgett Martin. The Martins paid $163, the Buckleys $60.

Today's plots sell for $420 to $985. ''I must soon buy a plot before they become too dear,'' said Fitzpatrick. Holy Cross also charges $652.20 for use of the chapel, transportation and excavation.

Despite their often-elaborate statuary and perpetual-care funds, cemeteries are neither spiritually nor legally forever. The Colma complex was developed in 1937 when, after 60 years of debate, the San Francisco Board of Supervisors ordered that all graveyards inside the cramped city be moved. The task was not completed until 1948, when the last of the estimated 100,000 bodies had been removed and thousands of headstones dumped into the Bay near the east jetty of the St. Francis Yacht Harbor.

There are non-Catholics buried at Holy Cross, and there are similar exceptions at other area cemeteries.

Western marshal Wyatt Earp is buried at the Jewish Hills of Eternity. The lawman was not Jewish; his wife was.

★ ★ ★

By mid-morning, the silence of the cemetery was broken as caravans of cars arrived for the first of the day's services. A black limousine drove slowly up the road near the gravesite, slowing but not stopping.

''Family,'' said Hickey. ''They will not stop, rarely do. Some come over to ask questions. They never talk about the person to be buried. You try to sympathize but there is really not much to say.''

The schedule does not call for a gravesite service. Most funerals, they explained, conclude at the chapel. By late morning, the trench was a bit more than five feet deep and the diggers, now working in very hard ground, decided they had gone down far enough. The traditional six-foot grave is an approximation and not legally required.

A supervisor with a walkie-talkie came over, surveyed the scene and told them the casket would be brought over before lunch. The men dropped an open redwood box into the hole, designed to fit around the coffin.

Soon after, a station wagon pulled up. Six other employees dragged a steel coffin, covered with a single wreath, from the back, and trundled it across the grass, a trail of white petals in their wake.

They paused but a moment to wrap two straps about the coffin, then dropped it quickly and without ceremony into the pit. The task took no longer than 30 seconds. The men walked off, chatting amiably, toward another job.

''At first I wasn't used to it,'' explained Fitzpatrick, standing off to the side. ''It was hard sometimes, particularly with children and young people, and I often nearly weeped myself. Now, I have seen so many of them. . . .''

Hickey took off his hat, sweater and jacket. "The work is hard. You don't have time to think about death," he said.

DISCUSSION

There is no ancient gentleman but gardeners, ditchers and grave-markers: They hold up Adam's profession.
—*Hamlet*, Act V, Scene I

Literary feature writing offers the newspaper writer an opportunity to take what might be seen as a mundane assignment and to raise it to a level of storytelling. Shinoff does that at the article's beginning, in which he describes the work of the men, not as they might have told him about it later but as it is happening. Shinoff makes the reader a witness to the work of gravediggers. He uses scene rather than summary, which allows the reader to watch the action take place.

Shinoff, although he remains the teller of the story, shifts his approach from literary to expository when he provides some history on gravediggers and cemeteries in San Francisco. Among other things, this enables him to write a compact story. A literary feature story does not have to be long.

Shinoff downplays his technique, attributing the final story form to the material. Shinoff is a reporter first and believes that if the reporting is not well done, nothing can save the story. "When the right material is assembled," he says, "it writes itself. Sure a good writer can fudge and play a bit, but I am tied to the material." To Shinoff, "form best reflects the subject," and although he is saying that to downplay his effort, the fact remains that not every story lends itself to literary treatment. Further, Shinoff place great weight on thorough reporting, and that too is a recurring effort behind the literary journalism in this book. Shinoff spent 1½ days reporting the story and another 1½ days writing and polishing.

Look at some of his polished writing. Shinoff uses similes (italicized) to give the reader another way of seeing the action.

He and Hickey drew their spaces across the plot, cutting the thick sod into 18 squares, *as neatly as a parent dividing a birthday cake*.
Working side by side, Fitzpatrick and Hickey then thrust their flat spades under the sod squares, lifting them off *like pancakes from a grill*.

To explain his writing technique, Shinoff reaches into his past.

I put in seven years as a construction worker—and a few more in related trades— before I was ever paid as a writer. Once I built a lot of houses, now I build stories. The site is owned by the publisher. I have a general idea of what I wish to build but the material is gathered in the reporting. After that it's all framing. If the lede [lead] doesn't work, just like an entranceway, it can be knocked down and built again. Sections can be enlarged, shortened; the trim comes last.

That may sound mechanical, but the analogy is apt, and the good writer recognizes how a story is constructed from basic materials. But first the good writer makes a blueprint, then follows the plan until the story is constructed. So Shinoff's claim that the story wrote itself belies the analysis aforethought that he put into the story.

This story begins not with the lead, but with the editor's note, which explains the story's intent. Think of the editor's note as prologue, an introduction. From there, Shinoff paints the opening scene. He then provides two paragraphs of background and description—an expository digression—before returning to the opening scene. The two paragraphs are needed to add information about the story's main characters. After the opening scene, the reader will want to know more about Fitzpatrick and Hickey, and Shinoff satisfies that interest with a brief digression.

When Shinoff makes an abrupt break in the story, he uses space breaks, in his case, three stars. Shinoff's first break takes the reader from the opening scene to an extended exposition of background on gravediggers in general and the two gravediggers in the story. The first exposition is followed by a second, also marked with a space break. The second exposition is half as long as the first. Shinoff does not want to get too far away from the main story.

Shinoff returns to the opening scene by picking up the action in mid-morning. By returning to the opening scene, Shinoff is tying the action back to its origin. This ensures continuity, which any good story must have. Cutting back to the opening scene propels the story forward. Shinoff finishes the story by showing how casually the coffin is placed into the grave, a contrast with the care the two gravediggers applied in digging the grave.

Another comparison can be made with the two gravediggers in Shakespeare's *Hamlet*. Shakespeare chose to present the gravediggers as clowns and show them as casual and unaffected by death. Hamlet complains to Horatio:

Has this fellow no feeling of his business, that he sings at grave-making?
    Horatio: Custom hath made it in him a property of easiness.
    Hamlet: 'Tis e'en so; the hand of little employment hath the daintier sense.

And what does the gravemaker sing while gravemaking?

A pick-axe, and a spade, a spade,
For and a shrouding sheet:
O, a pit of clay for to be made
For such a guest is meet.

Shinoff's gravediggers are compassionate by comparison.

A final note about the subject matter, which, as noted before, plays a part in whether a story can be written in a literary fashion. Shinoff says that of the stories in this series, the one that worked least well is that of the engineer—"what he did was too interesting. I got lost in the romance of it and didn't spend enough time on the basics—like how he blew the whistle.'' In other words, he forgot to gather detail.

"Details make a difference," Shinoff says. Look at the detail in this story. Sod cut into 18 squares. Gravediggers heavily muscled. Fitzpatrick, tall and ruddy with thick white hair. Hickey with dark hair that has streaks of sun-bleached blond. As the sun rises and the digging gets harder because of harder ground, the well bundled gravediggers begin removing layers of clothes.

Shinoff had a problem in another story because the subject of the story was not very articulate. Being inarticulate does not necessarily rule a person out of a literary feature piece, but it certainly places a greater reporting burden on the journalist.

For this story, Shinoff had a problem finding a cemetery that would cooperate. Shinoff said:

> Employers are often cautious of labor reporters. We often appear in the midst of disputes, which are often times when they would prefer to have no publicity at all. And by the nature of our trade, they often believe we are secretly in league with the unions. Unions, on the other hand, believe we are often bought by employers.

The problems so common to daily journalism can spill over in to the literary journalist's assignments.

* * *

> *Second Clown*: 'Who builds stronger than a mason, a shipwright or a carpenter?'
> *First Clown*: Ay, tell me that, and unyoke.
> *Second Clown*: Marry, now I can tell.
> *First Clown*: To't.
> *Second Clown*: Mass, I cannot tell.
> *First Clown*: Cudgel thy brains no more about it, for your dull ass will not mend his pace with beating; and when you are asked this question next say 'a grave-maker:' the houses that he makes last till doomsday.

Chapter Six
Farmers Harvest Fruit of Bountiful Summer

BACKGROUND

The first cool day of fall reminded a *Washington Post* editor that it was time for a change-of-season story, a traditional piece at many newspapers. "Rather than writing about how all the bureaucrats changed their cotton pin-stripes for ones of wool, [the editor] thought it would be interesting to explore the change of seasons in an environment where man is conscious of nature, where the relationship between the two is a vital factor," Mike Sager says. Sager went to Culpeper, Virginia, and eventually to the farm of Greg and Doris Smith. Sager spent 2 days reporting the story and at least 2 days writing. The resulting story was published in tandem with another about the changing season in Maryland and underneath a photograph from the Smith farm.

BIOGRAPHY

Mike Sager graduated from Emory University with a bachelor of arts degree in history and a minor in English. At Emory, he was an editor and columnist for the school's weekly newspaper and editor of a literary magazine and an underground campus guide. In his senior year, he worked for an alternative weekly in Atlanta. He attended the Georgetown Law Center in Washington for 3 weeks, then quit and joined the *Post* as a copyboy. Approximately 1 year later the *Post* hired him as a night police reporter. After assignments in general news and feature, he became a " 'Virginia rover,' assigned to wander Virginia and cover news, features and politics." He left the *Post* in the fall of 1983 and subsequently wrote for *Rolling Stone*,

GQ, *Playboy*, *Manhattan Inc.*, *Washingtonian*, and *Regardies*. He became a contributing writer to the new *Washington Post* Sunday magazine in January 1988.

THE STORY

Change of Season Comes to Bay Island, Va. Countryside
Farmers Harvest Fruit
of Bountiful Summer

(Monday, October 5, 1981.
© 1981 *The Washington Post*)

By Mike Sager
Washington Post Staff Writer

CULPEPER, Va.—The dawn is chill inside the barn, and Greg Smith's breath hangs in the air like puffs from a hand rolled smoke. A Holstein stands motionless before him, and he strokes the cow's black and white face with a rough, stained hand. A few steps away, the sun outlines the open barn door on the earth, and there summer lingers, warm to the skin.

It is autumn, harvest time at Ashland Farm. And while Smith still rises, with the certainty of the chime, at 5:30 sharp, the sun dawdles 60 seconds more each morning and moves imperceptibly to the south. Smith pulls a handful of brown corn silage from the trough, stirring the kernels and the chopped pieces of cob, stalk and shuck with a finger. He closes his hand tightly. When it opens again, the coarse, fluffy matter springs back to size. Perfect. The right amount of moisture to last through winter.

It has been a good year at Smith's 1,112-acre dairy farm, so bountiful that the feed crops he grew in his fields—the corn, barley, alfalfa and soybeans—have filled all five of his 60-foot silos. This year, he has had to buy two enormous white plastic bags to hold the extra bounty. They rest, bloated, in front of his clapboard farmhouse like two 50-yard caterpillars, gorged and sleeping off their feast.

A year ago, Smith was not so pleased. Drought had withered the crops, and food for his 750 head of cattle barely lasted the winter. Fewer cows and steers could be bred, less milk produced. Through that summer, he had matched his Heinzman travelling irrigation gun against the heat, sending it rolling through the fields, the fine spray leaving rainbows over the manicured rows. Still, the crop was poor.

But that is history as time on the farm goes. It has been a good season, and nature's new fidelity can be measured in bushels. By noon, Smith, 41, his brother Ken, 38, and their five hired hands have reached the middle of their 15-hour day. They have fed and milked the cows, picked and shelled and dried corn, raked and baled alfalfa, planted rye and replaced a fuel pump and a tractor belt.

Ninety miles west of Washington, at the foot of the Blue Ridge Mountains, fall is a time to prepare for winter, when the ground and the ponds will freeze and life itself will seem to be suspended. The verdant countryside is fading, and the smell of mature Grimes Golden and Yellow Delicious apples hangs sweet in the crystal air. The sun is round and low, and light splashes now across the fields more like a spreading coat of varnish than summer's sheer garment of translucent silk. Soon, the cows will linger in the barn, favoring the warmth of their extra winter issue of straw and sawdust over the cool grass by the pond, shadowed in the afternoon by Mount Pony.

Greg Smith is a quiet man, one who usually wears his sentiment, like his work shirt, tucked tightly under his belt. But this day, in his rush, he still has time to see. "You see such a beautiful world," Smith says, "and you think, 'How can people not believe there's a God?' To see a calf born, to plant a seed in the spring and see corn and alfalfa grow up tall by fall . . ."

He doesn't finish. Instead, he climbs into his red pickup truck and drives the several hundred yards to the house, which once was a hospital for Confederate soldiers.

Inside, Greg's wife, Doris, is giving a covered-dish lunch. "Just a bunch of us girls getting together to eat and sit around gabbing," she says.

Doris is a hearty woman with a straight-faced wit that makes a person shake his head seriously until he realizes she is making fun. "I suppose you think we're going to feed you lunch," she says, her vowels as country-round as her shape, her smile signaling the jest. She hands a plate, and then one to her husband, who first takes off his blue Ashland Farms cap and aims it at a dowel on the wall. The cap falls and he eyes it a moment, then turns and accepts the plate. It already has been a long day.

In the dining room, he helps himself to food from casseroles in straw baskets; cheese and broccoli, hamburger and beans, sausage and cheese. He returns to the kitchen to eat.

With the coming of fall, the eight women spooning homemade peach cobbler and vanilla ice cream onto their plates no longer gather at Linda Stapleton's pool or go wading in the Rapidan River near Irma Peters' place. Except for rare occasions like this one, they are too busy. In the basement are hundreds of cans and jars of peas, lima beans, corn, tomatoes, freezer jellies and pickles that Doris has recently preserved. Hill onions in her quarter-acre garden, a few tomatoes and green peppers and two bushels of pears still await her attention.

These days, Doris must cook for three sittings of breakfast, one for Greg and herself, one for her two children and one for Greg's grandmother. She cooks two lunches, two dinners.

Besides these duties, a variation of which all the women perform, Dorothy Walker, a slight woman with a white sweater draped around her shoulders and buttoned at the neck, says she always is hurrying the 12 miles to town or the 30 miles to Fredericksburg for parts when a tractor or a combine breaks down. "It never fails that when I get there, I can't describe it and have to call home," she says.

Mostly, the women have been busy winterizing, securing the trapdoors of basement stairways, airing electric blankets, caulking windows, cleaning flues. Apples for cider, sauce and pie filling must be picked and, at night, after their husbands have set the propane corn dryers for one more load, there are tired arms and sore backs to be massaged.

With the exception of Rita Wells, whose favorite color is orange, none of the women at Doris' table likes fall much. They have more chores, as do their husbands. Beside the harvest, pipes must be wrapped against the freeze, behemoth John Deere tractors filled with antifreeze. The coats of the cows grow thick and their udders must be shaved to ensure that the milk is sanitary.

And fall precedes winter, which is a slow, gray, desolate time. "It's so quiet in winter," says Gay Duckett, another of Doris' friends. "The crickets are gone and you look out and all you see is bare trees and death."

At Ashland Farms, there are whispers that the coming cold will be long and deep. The caterpillars are furry and black. The walnuts, coated in their spongy green skins, and the hickory nuts, acorns and persimmons are unusually abundant; the foliage on the trees is thick.

The next time Doris Smith will go wading in the Rapidan River near Irma Peter's place, or her husband, Greg, will plant a seed and watch the corn grow tall, or the dawn will have no chill or the sun will lay a garment of silk across the fields is another world away.

DISCUSSION

A regular reader of *The Washington Post* would probably recognize a story by Mike Sager even if his byline were not affixed to it. Sager has a personal style. His writing and description are intentionally original. In a story about a father and son hunting, Sager (1981) begins: ''The sun glows orange as it dips behind the ridge, back-lighting a silken spider web, laying long hardwood shadows across the valley'' (p. 1). There is no mistaking Sager's style. In *Best Newspaper Writing 1981*, Roy Peter Clark (1981) said: ''An essential playfulness runs through the work of most good writers, a love for the language in which words hug and bump each other'' (p. 11). Sager's words do a lot of hugging and bumping. Consider the next-to-last paragraph of the story analyzed here:

At Ashland Farms, there are whispers that the coming cold will be long and deep. The caterpillars are furry and black. The walnuts, coated in their spongy green skins, and the hickory nuts, acorns and persimmons are unusually abundant; the foliage on the trees is thick.

Another of this story's most striking elements is the present tense. Typically, newspaper stories are written in the past tense because they are about an event in the past. Telling a story in the present tense has virtues. It brings the action closer to the reader and makes it more immediate. Sager uses the present tense to let the reader view the setting and the action as it unfolds. Sager also uses present tense because it allows him to switch to past tense when he wants to delineate time more clearly.

Here is a paragraph using past and past perfect tense.

Three bills had to be signed into law to have the reform proposal enacted. The president had signed two bills last week and yesterday put his signature onto the third.

Obviously, past and past perfect tenses show time differences, but the past perfect does not seem to separate itself as neatly from the past as the past does from the present. By using present tense and past, Sager can shift scenes or turn to a paragraph of background without using any typographical device such as space breaks.

Sager uses description effectively, affirming a comment made early in the century by Remy de Gourmont (West, 1952)

> If there were an art of writing, it would be nothing more or less than the art of feeling, the art of seeing, the art of hearing, the art of using all the senses, whether directly or through the imagination; and the new, serious method of a theory of style would be an attempt to show how these two separate worlds—the world of sensations and the world of words—penetrate each other. (p. 57)

Sager calls *description* ''an intentional stylistic device.'' Sounding like de Gourmont, Sager says: ''Because the story was meant to convey the feeling—as well as the pace and the specifics—of all on the farm, the piece lent itself easily to description of nature.''
Sager intentionally uses original phrasing.

> I try to incorporate various elements of description into one phrase or thought: the warm sun becomes 'the sun outlines the the open barn door on the earth, and there summer lingers, warm to the skin.' The readers learn that the sun is warm, but they are given the chance to feel it on their skin rather than just being told about it. They also get the picture of the barn door and its shadow. The sun isn't just up there in the sky. It is doing something—making shadows.

Sager devotes his reporting energies to getting the detail that will provide concrete images. '''Autumn' is an example of how we can give our black and white newspaper print canvas color,'' Sager says. The effect is a vignette.

The story, like others in this book, is rich with small scenes. Again and again, Sager allows an experience to unfold before the reader's eyes—for example, when he describes Greg Smith getting into his truck and going to the house where Doris Smith and her friends are having lunch. Sager takes the reader into the house and makes the reader feel as though he is standing on the edge of the scene as it occurs.

Metaphor plays a part in Sager's writing. To Sager, ''metaphor aids description. It is interpretive, but I try to interpret in such a way that a universal image is offered.'' At one point, Sager writes that Smith ''usually wears his sentiment, like his work shirt, tucked tightly under his belt.'' The universal image results because at one time or another the reader has worn a shirt and tucked it in. From that metaphor, Sager says, ''we learn something about the man while learning about what he wears.'' Leon Surmelian (1968) said: ''One fresh metaphor can elevate a page of prose to the level of literature'' (p. 230). The journalist looking to produce something journalistic and literary must be sensitive to enriching the story at hand, and metaphor is one of the literary devices the journalist can use.

In organizing a story, Sager claims he has no conscious plan. ''Basically, organization just kind of comes to the story,'' he says, pointing out that to him ''it always seems that one point logically follows another, though I am conscious of the act that I don't want to plunge headlong into the story line. I try to advance a few steps forward, take a step back for history, clarification or a relevant aside, and then proceed onward. This way, the readers are spiraled into the story, as they would be in a short story or novel.''

An examination of this story reveals Sager's organizational scheme. He provides a descriptive opening, one in which the reader can feel the air temperature. Then he drops in a couple of paragraphs of background before returning to the present. Description of Greg Smith follows and then Sager introduces Smith's wife, Doris. Sager's ''advance a few steps forward, take a step back for history, clarification or a relevant aside, and then proceed onward'' is evident throughout. Sager ends the story by mentioning that winter and then spring and summer lie ahead. He nudges the story into the future even though it has come to an end.

Chapter Seven
A Fire on the Mountain

BACKGROUND

This story was a long time coming. Gilbert M. Gaul conceived of the idea almost 2 years before the story appeared. In between, Gaul changed jobs, went from covering crime and corruption in the Anthracite coal mines of Pennsylvania to reporting about the casinos in Atlantic City, New Jersey. The miners involved in this story kept in touch, and Gaul did some research on mine inspections. When the federal government was not forthright enough, he obtained some of his information through the Freedom of Information Act. A year after conceiving the story, he decided to write it in a magazine format and find a publisher later. Thus, the story was written before Gaul returned to his old newspaper, *The Pottsville* (Pennsylvania) *Republican*, which published it.

BIOGRAPHY

Gilbert M. Gaul is a graduate of Fairleigh Dickinson University with a major in psychology and minors in English and history. He also received certification to teach from Montclair State College in New Jersey. He free-lanced for numerous newspapers and small magazines then went to work for the *Times-News* in Lehighton, Pennsylvania. After three years, he joined the staff of *The Pottsville Republican*. While there, he shared a Pulitzer Prize for special local reporting. He moved on to *The Bulletin* in Philadelphia (to cover Atlantic City) and then returned to the *Republican*. In 1982 he was chosen as a Nieman Fellow. In September of 1983, he joined the staff of the *Philadelphia Inquirer*.

THE STORY

A fire on the mountain:
The story of the Kintzel Brothers

(Friday, March 20, 1981.
© 1981 J. H. Zerbey Newspaper Inc.
All rights reserved.)

On a rinsed, cobalt blue morning, Harvey Kintzel and I climbed aboard his 1973 Ford pickup and started up a winding dirt road into the small coal hole he and his three brothers have scraped a living from for the last 23 years.

High atop of the mysteriously named Big Lick Mountain in Tremont Township, Schuylkill County, the land bristles in sudden bulges and creases where miners once gouged the earth, and then quickly descends into a thick, fortress-like mantle of trees. "Forgotten country," Kintzel, big and earnest, calls it. A clawed, forbidden land of sallow overgrowth, ghostly winter oaks and shuttered mines.

Where the dirt road finally levels out, a breach in the woods gives way to a narrow path leading into one of these abandoned mines, a small coal hole worked during the Depression when many of the large anthracite collieries shut down and the nation was just beginning its frenzied, inexorable love affair with oil.

Signs of decay are everywhere. Jutting above the muted overgrowth, poking out of an amorphous, shoulder-high mound of coal, shaping a steepled arabesque of corroded steel and rotted wood. Although the sun has barely reached this side of the mountain, several long steamy shafts of light stretch across the mouth of this forgotten mine into the nearby woods. The light seems to suggest nature might undo what it has taken 50 years to retrieve. But that would be impossible, of course, because the land near reclaims itself precisely, a fact Harvey Kintzel seems to recognize only too well.

"The mountain's plenty hard on a man up here," he says as we step back into his pickup after surveying the landscape. "Full of surprises and pain. I guess you could say we Kintzels have managed a truce with the mountain because we're still here and everybody else has left. But it's an uneasy truce just the same."

Steady, possessed of a grip that swallows ordinary hands and stained by 20 years in the mines, Harvey Kintzel, 51, is so much a product of the cramped, labyrinthine tunnels and methodical practices of this profession. When he speaks, his words are chosen carefully, interrupted only by the singsong lilt of his Pennsylvania Dutch heritage. His movements are similarly measured, honed from years of pacing himself and peeling away wasted motion. His approach is almost always friendly and direct.

Dressed in freshly-washed overalls, faded flannel shirt and a rumpled blue cap, Kintzel does not appear particularly large or rugged. But his baggy clothes are deceptive, hiding a solid figure better than six feet tall and 185 pounds. One easily imagines him having played guard or tackle on his high school football team. His forearms are immense, twice the size of my own, coiled from years of wielding the tools of his trade. From shoulders to waist he is cut like an inverted pyramid, from waist to shoetops like a tested oak, straight and true. His facial features are of a kind: square-jawed, symmetrical, unflinching. The only incongruous element, a wry smile that appears at the corners of his mouth whenever he becomes self-conscious.

"I've seen this land work on a grown man and force him to quit the business for an easier job," the son of a deacon who raised 11 children on a 38-acre farm in nearby Pine Grove says as he surveys the cruel landscape. "I don't think you could find anyone who knows say this isn't one of the toughest mountains around to mine. Nothing comes easy up here. But then if it did I suspect we wouldn't be nearly as stubborn ourselves. Everything has its way of evening out."

Kintzel fumbles with a pair of thick black glasses that fence in his pale, serious features. Then he starts the pickup, carefully backing it out to the dirt road that will now carry us to the brothers' mine. The ride is particularly bumpy; the road, slashed uneven and stained black from 80-odd years of coal being hauled over it.

There are an estimated seven billion tons of anthracite reserves in northeastern Pennsylvania, the only appreciable deposit of hard coal in the United States. Much of that coal is located in what is commonly referred to as the Southern Anthracite Field, a 48-mile band of coal that snakes through the Schuylkill, Dauphin and Lebanon counties. The best reserves, those that are easily recoverable and have a high BTU value, are concentrated in southern Schuylkill County near where the Kintzels mine, but as Harvey Kintzel quickly points out, "Not quite near enough."

The brothers—Harvey, Nathan, 57, Jesse, 55, and Ira, 49—work the north face of Big Lick Mountain, a sullen and frayed mass of earth that rises up quickly along Route 209 about 15 miles south of Pottsville. The particular area they mine was once heavily worked by the Lincoln Coal Company, a firm that employed upwards of 600 miners during its heyday in the 1920s. The company prospered until the Depression, then collapsed, but not before removing most of the coal in Big Lick Mountain.

Today the Kintzels work the same two veins of coal—the Lykens Nos. 6 & 7 veins— they started taking coal from more than 23 years ago. Mining these two veins is a little like trying to squeeze blood from a stone. The pitch is severe, even when one considers that coal rarely lies flat on its side in the anthracite fields. Thirty-eight degrees. About the same as looking up into the eyes of your dentist. On top of that, there really isn't all that much coal to speak of, and what is here requires and inordinate amount of work to remove.

The Lykens No. 6 vein averages about two feet in height with a maximum girth of six feet. The No. 7 rarely exceeds three feet at the working face. Both are sealed more than 700 feet beneath the icy face of Big Lick Mountain. Only a small independent outfit like the Kintzels could really afford to bother with these two veins, Harvey says. A large operator with expensive equipment and lots of miners would go bankrupt before he took his first 1000 tons coal to the breaker.

But using their well-honed manual techniques and lots of hard work, the brothers managed to survive, something many of the other small independents in the area cannot claim.

Once there were dozens of independent outfits like the Kintzels working on Big Lick. But one by one with the costs of mining escalating and coal becoming scarcer and scarcer, they left for the other mountains or other types of work. It is impossible to say how many exactly because no records are kept. But a best estimate based on piecing together an array of documents comprising the public record suggests a loss of at least 200 independent mines in Schuylkill County in the last dozen years. Many independents claim the number is closer to 300.

Today an estimated 75 independent mines operate in the county. But the number fluctuates from day to day depending on several factors, including when the federal mine inspectors are due for a visit. It is not uncommon for independents to close their shops if they know the inspectors are coming. Even more than the risk of injury, the independents fear the inspectors and their dreaded notepads in which they write down violations of the Federal Mine Health and Safety Act.

Kintzel slows his pickup while negotiating a particularly bumpy stetch of road, taking this time to describe one particularly illuminating tug-of-war between an independent and an unnamed inspector. The clash occurred several years ago and seemed to involve a question of territory and dominance. Each time the miner knew the inspector was coming, he closed his operation and went off to hide in the woods. The inspector, meanwhile, left notes. Where are you? When can I inspect your mine? Like that. The miner ignored all of them. It went on like that for months. A standoff. Finally, the inspector returned late one night and descended into the mine unannounced.

But before he left, he tacked up a list of 50 alleged violations, including one citation because the miner didn't have a place to change his clothes. Faced with paying fines for each of the violations or going out of business, the miner closed his shop and went home. The last anyone had heard he had gotten out of the business of mining coal.

"I was saying earlier how hard this mountain is," Kintzel repeats as he finishes this story. "Well it isn't just the mountain that is getting to these men. It's also these regulations and federal inspectors that are causing them to quit. There's too many of them and they're too severe. I know that for a fact because we Kintzels have seen it with our own eyes."

He then launches into a long, highly emotional attack against the inspectors and the federal government's program for mine safety, the thrust of which concerns itself with how inflexible the inspectors allegedly are and how the safety regulations are driving the independents out of business. "They have it fixed in their heads that they're the only ones who know anything about safety," Kintzel grouses. "But it just isn't so."

The tirade goes on. Always another question. Questions about intent. Questions about procedures. Questions about law. "Why are these regulations based on soft coal mining and not hard coal? Did you know that they can fine us without even giving us a chance to fix what is supposedly wrong? What I want to know is why we independents can't get the same due process of the law that everyone else is entitled to?"

All the while we are following the winding dirt road into the spot where the brothers work. The earth is steaming and mottled as we go along, cold on the surface, burning beneath, much the same as my host and the sudden fever come over him.

"As you can see, I get a might worked up whenever the subject of these regulations comes up," Kintzel says. "It's hard for an outsider to understand. But this is our livelihood, our bread and butter we're talking about. No man is going to give that up without a fight."

Kintzel falls silent again. We drive on. Across the hoary mountaintop. The sun is still not above the treeline and I can see my breath inside the pickup. Kintzel mentions that he hopes the weather holds. "Snow and ice are particularly hard on us," he says. "Everything slows down." After a while he pulls the pickup into a recess next to a small, weather-beaten shanty he and his three brothers use to change into their mining clothes. The roughly hewn structure seems a precarious fusion of wood and sheet metal. Scraps, really. I mention this to Kintzel, who agrees good-naturedly. "It isn't much, but it serves its purpose," he says matter-of-factly. That is the way it is with the brothers. If something works, they keep it. If something doesn't work, they quickly discard it. The margin of error in mining is slight at best. Wasted movement has no place. And there is little room for experimentation in the classical sense.

These lessons have carried over to the brothers' lives outside the mine as well, shaping everything from their impassive external features to the simple and consistent value system they live by. Nobody appears to meet us, but a light inside the shanty indicates the rest of the Kintzel brothers are already inside waiting. "Probably warming themselves," Harvey explains as we step outside into the cold December air again.

On a clear day you can look down the north face of Big Lick Mountain outside the Kintzels' makeshift shanty and see the Kocher Coal Company's Porter Tunnel operation where nine miners lost their lives March 1, 1977, during a sudden inrush of water outside the West Skidmore Gangway. Probers later determined that the water breached the gangway from nearby abandoned mine workings that did not appear on the firm's maps. Developed during the early 1930s, and later flooded when the mines were closed, those workings never were completely surveyed by Kocher officials, the probers alleged.

Unlike many independents, the Kintzels have never worked in a large underground mine like the Porter Tunnel, which employs 120 miners and operates two shifts. The choice is intentional, they will quickly tell you.

"I have no taste for working in a large mine, always answering to somebody else and never knowing what the miner on the previous shift might have done down there," explains Nathan Kintzel, both the smallest and the most experienced of the brothers. "Here at least we can control our own fate and keep an eye out for each other. I believe you lose that at a larger mine."

Disenchanted with the ways of the large mines, Nathan Kintzel opted for the more autonomous if financially less rewarding life of an independent miner, appearing on Big Lick Mountain 23 years ago at the age of 34. He arrived at the worst possible time, the dead of winter, but still intent on succeeding. The body and spirit were willing, he recalls today, the mountain less so. But slowly, using pick and shovel, blasting caps, and a faithful mule to haul in his timber, Nathan Kintzel carved a four-foot-high, six-foot-wide hole 720 feet into the guts of this stingiest of mountains.

The enormity of that experience shaped Nathan's way of thinking about work and life, his brothers recall today, resulting in the quiet but firm demeanor that suggests another, easier way of earning a living would be unwelcomed, probably unprincipled.

"Nate has always been the one we look to for leadership," Harvey explains to me as we head into the shanty. "You won't ever see it or hear it from him because he's not a braggart, but pound for pound there isn't a better miner or steadier person around. Even the federal inspectors with whom he has battled for years will tell you as much."

The cluttered shanty is filling up with smoke as we enter. Inside the three brothers are huddled around an ancient looking coal-fired stove. It is here each morning before they descend into their mine that gossip and ritual converge in the slow discarding of sleep. "Like anyone, we too, procrastinate a little," Harvey quips.

This morning the brothers are more animated than usual and go to great lengths to explain to their visitor how the inspectors from the Federal Mine Safety and Health Administration (MSHA) are slowly forcing them and other independent miners out of business—or so they believe.

"These laws—passed in 1969 and amended in 1977—were designed to prevent danger to the lives of employees working in large mining operations,'' Nathan Kintzel winces. ''But we don't have any employees. All we have is ourselves, and we aren't about to risk our lives just to make a few extra dollars.''

''If I choose to have an unsafe home I am constitutionally protected, am I not?'' queries Harvey. ''But the federal government is saying because I am a miner I don't have the same rights, that the Constitution doesn't apply to me. Like I was saying earlier, they seem to have two separate sets of laws, one for miners and one for everybody else.''

Attorneys for the Kintzels and other independents have attempted to use this argument—thus far unsuccessfully—in some of the dozens of lawsuits that MSHA officials have brought against them for ignoring federal mining regulations. But in rulings that to date have reached as high as the Third Circuit Court of Appeals, the federal courts have interpreted the Mine Safety and Health Act to apply equally to all mines, large and small, surface and underground.

''Isn't that the silliest thing you ever heard?'' Nathan asks as we huddle close to the fire to warm ourselves. ''I believe the federal government must have gone blind from writing so many citations on us small operators to have arrived at such a conclusion.''

The brothers begin changing into their mining clothes, thickly soiled overalls that are either black or colored black from coal. It is impossible to tell which. Hardhats with single mantis-like lights. Safety lamps for measuring methane gas that are attached at the waist. Work boots covered with mud and grime.

While we are waiting for Ira—the youngest but largest Kintzel—to fix his safety lamp, Harvey removes a stack of manuals from a nearby chair and brushes off a thick layer of dust. ''This here is just one of our problems with the federal law,'' he explains, handing over a collection of soft cover manuals that must be half-a-foot thick. ''As you can see, these books were meant for mines with an office staff just to fill them out, for large bituminous mines, not for us small independent operators.''

The manuals include pre-shift and on-shift daily reports; reports on the condition of hoisting equipment; weekly exams for methane gas and hazardous conditions; exams of emergency escapeways and reports on electrical equipment.

The manuals seem upon reflection an appropriate symbol of the brothers' frustrations with the federal laws regulating their mine. Intricate, arcane, even academic. In a word, everything the brothers aren't. In 1978, they were cited for failing to keep these records up to date. More incredibly, they say, they were also cited because the manuals they did use were not of an approved type.

''If we filled all of these books out completely, we wouldn't have any time left to go mining,'' Nathan concludes.

''Only half of these reports are even needed,'' adds Jesse.

''How do you manage?'' the brothers are asked.

''Let's just say we are practicing some civil disobedience,'' Nathan says with a faint smile. The brothers laugh, sharing their private joke on the federal regulators, and then the smoky room falls quiet again.

''When I fought in the war (World War II under General George Patton) I believed I was fighting to make this country free,'' Nathan, the first to speak again, says thoughtfully. ''Now I see that wasn't so. You're never really free, not even in this country.'' These words are not spoken bitterly. They seem rather a carefully measured reflection of what has been lost.

"If we were free, these federal inspectors would leave us alone," Ira, strong and reserved, assures his brother.

"If we were free," Nathan, in turn concludes, "the federal inspectors would come only when we needed them and not when they pleased."

"Amen to that," agrees Harvey.

"Amen."

• • •

Before descending into their mine for the day, the brothers are paid a visit by Clarence B. Miller, a retired state mine inspector who probably knows the Kintzels and their mining procedures as well as anyone.

"Imminent danger is everywhere on earth," Miller, a short, puffy-faced man with 49 years mining experience says when asked to assess the safety of the Kintzels' mine. "You can't go in one of these mines and not find something you wouldn't consider dangerous. Mining is dangerous by nature and most of these fellas are no fools about that. The Kintzels, I would say, are more careful than most."

"The federal law has 3,000 regulations in it and there's still accidents," quickly adds Harvey. "You know, you can add another 3,000 regulations but you'll still have accidents. The reason is that you can't eliminate human error in these mines; that's something you just can't legislate."

"There are careful miners and there are fools," Nathan points out.

"That's right," the brothers agree.

"If you communicate with these federal inspectors even they will tell you privately that they don't agree with the Act entirely, especially as it is applied to these independents," Clarence Miller explains. "But almost in the same breath they will tell you that there's nothing they can do about it, that their hands are tied or that their supervisors are breathing down their necks."

"I am told that the federals have to meet a quota (of violations)," Harvey Kintzel suggests. "It's a bounty system."

Miller says that he does not know about this.

"I've heard it," Kintzel repeats. "I'm not saying it's so, but I wouldn't be surprised."

"Nothing would surprise me about the federals," Nathan says tartly.

"They are like a lot of—how should I say?—school children let out at the end of the day the way they roam through these hills looking for trouble," Harvey concludes.

After awhile the conversation jumps to the energy crisis and the stranglehold the large anthracite operators hold over the industry.

"You know it's one of the greatest ironies that we have this here energy shortage at a time we independents can't afford to stay in the business," Harvey Kintzel tells us. "I blame the federal government for that. There wouldn't be an energy shortage if they just took some of these ropes away that they have tied around our necks."

"On the one hand they're saying we've got to have more coal, and on the other they're putting us out of business—it doesn't make any sense," Nathan agrees.

"I believe they may want us out of business," Harvey suggests.

"Look at the way we little operators are treated. We're the only ones going out of business. I think the federal government has decided that it wants to turn control of the coal fields over to a few."

When he is questioned about this, Kintzel retreats slightly but holds to his basic premise. "I have no proof of this exactly. But if you look at what's happening, I believe you'll see a pattern. The only ones going out of business are the independents, the small guys, while the big operators just seem to be getting richer and richer. I don't believe that's by accident either.''

"Like you said before, we're easy targets,'' Nathan assures his brother.

"Nobody cares about the independents,'' Jesse murmurs.

"It's a conspiracy is what I think—put all of your eggs in one basket,'' Nathan says.

"If you ask me, it's true,'' Harvey nods in agreement.

• • •

During a telephone conversation with John B. Shutack, MSHA's anthracite supervisor for mine safety, I raised the Kintzels' concerns about a conspiracy between the federal government and the large operators.

"It just isn't true,'' the veteran administrator said. "There is no conspiracy. We enforce the laws evenly across the board.''

Did he have any ideas why the brothers would have arrived at such a conclusion?

"I can only guess,'' Shutack said. "I suspect they're concerned because so many of these small operators appear to be going out of business. Maybe they believe they're being picked on or singled out? But like I said, it's just not so. The laws, granted, have had some effect on these fellas, but they're certainly not the only factor to come into play. In my opinion, most of these independent operators have failed because of the general decline of the industry over the last 40 years. The entire industry has suffered greatly.

"If we were being hard-nosed or pig-headed, that would be one thing. But we aren't,'' Shutack, a big, sturdily-built man with likeable ways, said. "We're doing the job the Congress wanted us to do. I would be the first to admit that these laws are a burden to the independents sometimes. But we do try to work with these men when we can find some common ground. That's the key in my opinion. We really do want to help. But if we can't find that room to work together then we'll meet them through whatever position we have to, whether that's through the courts or wherever.''

• • •

"Common ground'' is a phrase that regularly slips in and out of John Shutack's sentences. It is as if he were a labor mediator rather than a mine safety regulator, and in a way that's true. Shutack is frequently called in to restore peace between the independents and his inspectors. Sometimes that means making a phone call, sometimes throwing himself directly into the fray.

In the summer of 1979 I sat in on a meeting between Shutack and about 30 independents at the American Legion Hall in Pine Grove. Under constant attack from the miners, Shutack managed to keep his composure and defend his inspectors. The expression "common ground'' appeared often in his speech that day. "If you are willing to work with us, find some common ground, I think there's room enough for both of us to do our thing,'' he said. By the end of the often riotous session Shutack had not converted many of the independents to his side, but he had gained the respect of more than one.

"I think he's caught in a bind,'' Harvey Kintzel said as we descended into the hot summer afternoon again. "He's got a job to do and he has to do it. You can't fault a man for that. It's just that the law's all wrong.''

During a 41-month period from 1970-1973, Shutack's inspectors visited the Kintzels' mine on Big Lick Mountain 84 times, issuing 32 citations, including some allegedly so serious that they ordered the mine closed.

Still other citations, like a 1972 notice the brothers received for not having an on-site bathing facility, clearly left the Kintzels more than just a little perturbed.

"That citation is a perfect example of how the law puts a burden on the small operator," Nathan Kintzel says sharply. "A large operator with hundreds of miners can afford to put in a bathing facility. But for the little man it's impossible. It's the difference between staying in business and going broke."

"If I want to take a bath, I can go home any time I want and take one," adds Harvey impatiently. "Before you know it the inspectors will want to cite us for not being clean shaven in the morning."

One of the Kintzels' biggest complaints about the federal regulations is that each citation, no matter how trivial, automatically carries a fine, from as little as $14 to as high as $10,000. Miners may appeal their fines, and many ultimately succeed in having them lowered, but as Harvey Kintzel notes, "It's the principle of the thing that most disturbs us."

"They have too broad a power," adds Nathan. "They fine you first and negotiate later. It should be the other way around."

The other way around is the way state mine inspectors from the Department of Environmental Resources operate—bargaining first and fining later. The Kintzels seem to agree with this approach. "There's room to breathe," Harvey says simply. "Most any man if given a little time will cooperate with the inspectors. I've got no complaints about the state (inspectors)."

Tensions betwen the Kintzels and MSHA officials came to a head in May 1973 when federal inspector Dean Updegrave ordered their mine closed following a routine inspection. According to a copy of the inspection report filed in Shutack's office, Updegrave uncovered a section of loose roofing inside the Kintzel mine that allegedly posed the brothers "imminent danger." The trouble, as described in the report, was caused by rotted and broken timber supports in a section of the main gangway where the Kintzels have worked the Lykens Nos. six and seven veins for 23 years. Updegrave ordered the brothers to close shop until they repaired the roofing. The Kintzels, in turn, showed the inspector out of their mine.

"None of us is so smart he can't stand a little advice," Harvey Kintzel says to me more than six years after Updegrave's findings. "But that man wasn't offering us advice. He was ordering us around as if we didn't have enough sense to replace some bad wood. Writing us up as he did without giving us a chance to fix those props just put us in a corner. We didn't have any choice but to fight back."

Listening carefully to this exchange, Nathan Kintzel suddenly adds: "We fixed those props all right, after he left. But we didn't do it because of him. We did it in spite of him."

When they ejected Updegrave from their mine, the Kintzels drew a line between themselves and the federal government that was not be be crossed for the better part of five years. In the minds of the brothers civil war had been declared and the federal inspectors were on the wrong side of the issue. Thus when Updegrave and a fellow inspector returned in June 1973 to reinspect the Kintzels' mine, the brothers denied them entry. "We told them that we were no longer participating in the federal government's program," Harvey says. Another attempt to inspect the mine in July was similarly rebuffed, prompting MSHA official James R. Laird to write in a memo: "The principal contention of the operators was that they were not financially able to comply with this law, much of which was too inapplicable for their small operation, but they had to make a living somehow . . . therefore, there was no sense permitting us to go into the mine.''

From March 1974 until September 1977, MSHA simply ignored the Kintzels' mine. ''That's one I could never understand,'' muses Harvey Kintzel. ''If there was danger inside our mine like they said there was, why did they allow us to continue working there? Why did they wait so long to take us into court on the charges?''

But Shutack says that additional inspection attempts would have been futile. ''We had tried to inspect their mine and they wouldn't let us in. They had made up their minds. I'm satisfied we did everything we could.''

In September 1977 MSHA officials finally decided to attempt another inspection. The reasoning is not all together clear. But documents in the case suggest that attorneys in the Department of Labor's legal division wanted to know what the status of the case was. In any event, the inspectors were rebuffed once more. ''Nate told them that the conditions remained the same as before,'' Harvey Kintzel recalls. Once again, the inspectors disappeared from Big Lick Mountain.

Finally, in February 1978 the brothers received notice that they were to appear before Judge Edward Cahn in Federal District Court in Allentown to explain why they shouldn't be held in contempt of the Mine Safety and Health Act for refusing to allow inspections.

The Kintzels came with their attorney and argued that their mine was their home and as such exempt from unwarranted intrusions by the federal inspectors. But as has been the case in all of the independents' trials to date, the miners lost, Judge Cahn ruling that the Mine Safety and Health Act required the brothers to allow inspections on at least four occasions a year, more frequently if the inspectors thought there was a need.

Negotiations between attorneys for the Kintzels and MSHA followed and on Feb. 24 the brothers reluctantly allowed several inspectors inside their cramped operation for the first time in nearly five years.

The inspectors promptly wrote the Kintzels up for 42 alleged safety violations. But somewhat surprisingly the ''imminent danger'' citation, the match that had ignited the five-year battle between the brothers and the federal government, was not included in this new list. Although the bulge in the roofing of the main gangway still remained, the Kintzels had retimbered the area, apparently leading the inspectors to reason that the problem had been corrected.

Now whenever Harvy Kintzel takes a visitor into his mine, he makes a point of showing him the bulge. ''It has been threatening our lives since 1973,'' Kintzel says with no small amount of sarcasm.

''In hindsight, there was clearly a lack of communication between our inspectors and the Kintzels,'' John Shutack says when asked to assess the volatile relationship between the brothers and MSHA. ''We probably could have have done a better job of listening to each other. But often these guys feel like they're being put in a corner and they're really too close to the situation to respect what our position is. You have to be willing to look for some common ground in order to make this work.''

Since 1978, Shutack says, the Kintzels have been a model of cooperation and their mine has generally been in compliance with the law. Harvey Kintzel smiles when advised of these remarks. ''If we are in compliance now,'' he ways, ''we were in compliance then. We're not doing anything so different today.'' MSHA records seem to support his claim. Of the 42 alleged violations uncovered during the 1978 inspection, only 22 were found to be corrected during reinspection five months later. Shutack says inspectors have been able to work with the Kintzels more since the 1978 negotiations.

Harvey Kintzel thinks that publicity the brothers have received in recent years has made the inspectors more cautious. "Without that, I sometimes wonder whether we would still be in in business," he says.

• • •

Harvey Kintzel estimates the brothers split $36,000 after expenses in 1979 for their labors inside their small mine. That figure is based on mining an average of 55 tons of coal a week, with the raw (unprocessed) coal sold at a nearby breaker for $24-a-ton. A few of the independents—but not many—have fared better. Most earn in the neighborhood of what the Kintzels take home. Clearly nobody is getting rich.

"A lot of folks don't understand how we can make such a sacrifice on our families when we could probably be working regular jobs somewhere else," Kintzel says as we maneuver along the dark, narrow gangway inside the brothers' mine. "I believe that is the hardest question we have to answer because it strikes the closest to home."

To make ends meet, three of the Kintzels' wives work in a nearby apparel factory, earning about $10,000-a-year. Harvey cuts corners by raising his own beef and keeping several cows for milk at his 38-acre farm in Pine Grove. His work schedule sometimes reads like that of a chief executive officer of a large corporation—without the big salary and perks.

Up at six a.m. to milk the cows, then off to Big Lick to work a full shift in the mine, and home again to take care of the chores that have a way of continually backing up on a working farm. During seasons when there is planting or harvesting to do, he occasionally leaves the mine early. But the mine routinely comes first. "It's our bread and butter," the father of five says matter-of-factly.

Like the mines their predecessors worked during the Depression, the Kintzel's operation is a throwback to a time when manual techniques dominated the industry. Their method of mining is deceptively simple. Drive a chute into a pitched seam of coal varying in thickness from inches to several feet, then slowly let the coal gravitate toward the miner, who shovels it into a one-ton buggy which he pushes by hand to the gangway entrance and dumps into the same hoist that carried him into the mine. The coal is hauled out via a steel cable, the hoist returns a few minutes later empty, and the whole process begins all over again.

You won't find any signs of the modern technology that has revolutionized underground mining inside the Kintzels' operation. The brothers can neither afford it nor feel they have a need for it. They work instead using explosives to open their holes into the vein, hand-held electric drills to carve out a working face at the seam, and picks and shovels when working in particularly stubborn corners, of which there are more than a few in their tightly cut mine.

"Like I was saying earlier, this here is an obsolete way of mining," Harvey Kintzel ventures without embarrassment. "The costs to a large operator coming in here with a lot of men and expensive machinery wouldn't be worth it because there's not enough coal. So they lease it to us. And because we're just stubborn enough or maybe dumb enough, we try to make a go of it. But I'm not complaining. For us Kintzels, the mountain suits our needs just fine. We can earn a decent living here if the federal inspectors will just leave us alone."

Hunched over to avoid banging our heads, we press along. At one point we pass a torn, sullied sheet hanging incongruously from the ceiling of the tunnel down to the floor. This is a vestige of another run-in with the inspectors, Kintzel explains. "They said we weren't getting enough air flow down here . . . and needed a way of channelling the air in order to be in compliance with the law. So we put up this sheet and then they didn't bother us no more."

The lamps from our headgear bounce off the handmade trolley tracks the Kintzels put down to push their buggy along. The 1¼ inch tracks are made of iron and raise ever so slightly so that the buggy, when loaded, will gravitate toward the gangway entrance, where the coal is hoisted to the surface. "Without some sort of grade it would be near impossible to push the buggy a half-mile with all that coal in it," Kintzel says. "What we have here is a miniature railway, a way of saving ourselves some time and energy."

The Kintzels have driven 50-odd chutes into the Lykens number six and seven veins in the 23 years they have worked this mine. In a way it is hard to imagine these two veins, which are relatively small as anthracite veins go, would have any coal left in them. But they do. Enough to keep the Kintzels going another 10 years if necessary. But the brothers have another plan, which they have already begun putting into operation.

Near the end of the gangway where the Lykens six and seven pinch out—are interrupted by impenetrable stone—the Kintzels have tunnelled above and around the interruption to another section of the Lincoln Colliery's former workings. There they will be able to mine what by and large amounts to a virgin area of coal. And if all goes according to plan, the Kintzels say, they will work in this new section until they retire sometime in the next decade.

On another trip to Big Lick Mountain, Harvey Kintzel took me to see this new section. Like their other mine, we reached the new workings by hoist, descending at a 38-degree angle into the mountain. The smell of fresh timber punctuated the damp air as we were lowered 550 feet through the darkness. The plan, Harvey explained as we inched along, was to continue driving their slope another 100 feet, where they would then cut a gangway paralleling the Lykens number seven as it starts up again after its stony interruption. He estimated they were at least a year away from finishing the gangway. In the interim, they continued blasting and digging their way deeper into the mountain, laying new tracks and hoisting out a mixture of coal and slate as they inched along.

"Right now we're taking out about 45 tons of coal a week, give or take a few tons," Kintzel said. "When we reach a point we can start working in honest after we get our gangway done, we'll be more likely to double our take up to 100 tons a week. That's not bad mining for a small hole like this. That's not bad at all."

Instead of riding back out of the new mine in the hoist, Kintzel suggested we climb out so he could show me a small gangway that was formerly part of the Lincoln Colliery, into which Nathan Kintzel had tunnelled many months earlier when the brothers were just beginning their search for a new area to mine. Climbing several hundred feet up a 38-degree pitch in semi-darkness is no small task for an experienced miner, but still infinitely more difficult for someone who isn't used to maneuvering in such cramped confines.

Miners, I rapidly observed, are a lot like mountain climbers, in an inverted sort of way, relying heavily on a sixth sense of knowing precisely when to shift their weight and use the mountain to their advantage. Kintzel led the way up. Using the same wooden rails for support that the hoist rides, he moved quickly and effortlessly ahead. Much faster than a 51-year-old who had suffered a heart attack should be able to, I reasoned. By contrast, I struggled along, probably too cautiously because at several junctures I had to call Kintzel to wait until I caught up to him.

At the 250-foot level, we left the track and wedged our way under an overhanging ledge into a much larger, arched tunnel. This was the gangway section Nathan Kintzel had found months before using an old map of the Lincoln Colliery mines. From all appearances the company had been exploring in the area when it ceased operations. The gangway stopped just about where the coal began. But other than a few test holes, there were no signs active mining had ever taken place here.

Compared to the Kintzels' operation, this tunnel was almost spacious. We could stand upright without any trouble and the width was at least four or five bodies across. The ceiling was cut like an entranceway to a cathedral and was shrouded in as many shadows. Holy this hole was not, however. Painted on one of the walls was a message from an unidentified miner to an associate: "Victor is a bull-thrower." Victor left no reply.

Using small fragments of rock found nearby, we chipped away at the walls of the tunnel, which Kintzel then pronounced to be jackstone, a local expression for a low grade type of coal that is a mixture of anthracite and shale. Here and there a tiny seam of anthracite no more than an inch or two thick snaked through these walls like the rings of a tree trunk. The closer you got to the Kintzels' new slope, the thicker these seams became, suggesting coal was just around the corner, which was literally true. Nathan Kintzel had guessed as much before even laying eyes on the Lincoln Gangway, reasoning that the presence of the miners in the area indicated they had been exploring for coal. He had not been wrong either. But before he could be certain he first had to wend his way 500 feet through darkness and stone, blasting and cutting a tunnel from the Kintzels' old mine up to the gangway. Nathan had relied on a map purchased from the brothers' landlord, Karl Goos, a local stripminer, as his guide. Also, 23 years of mining experience inside Big Lick Mountain. Slowly, like a mole in search of a winter meal, he punched through to the floor of the old Lincoln Colliery gangway and saw the handwriting on the wall. Coal, he reasoned, couldn't be very far behind.

• • •

We finally catch up with Nathan Kinzel on our return trip down the gangway. He is leaning on a shovel as we approach, face smudged, watching his larger brother Ira put the finishing touches on a buggy-load of coal. After another shovel or two, Ira leans down and gives the buggy a push. Slowly, painfully, it starts forward and he hops aboard, tucking down on a narrow sideboard. The buggy picks up speed and Ira disappears into the darkness. A human cannonball. A few moments later, we hear thick, unencumbered laughter in the distance, then pieces of a song. "We do have some fun down here," Nathan says with a smile.

Harvey Kintzel and I begin the long walk back to the hoist, bending low to avoid the ceiling and props, sloshing through the puddles and grime. Kintzel maneuvers his large body through these tight spaces with surprising alacrity, ducking here and bending there just at the right moment. We pass the location of the by now infamous "imminent danger" without a word. But later while waiting for the hoist, Kintzel reflects again: "What we Kintzels are fighting about, you know, is really a way of life. We've been up here for years mining without any problems. The trouble didn't start until they passed that law and the inspectors came up here. Before that we were free men. Like Nate says, a man could succeed or fail on the results of his own labors. Now we don't have that. This other ingredient has clouded the picture, so to speak. The only thing certain is we are no longer free.

"I suspect a lot of people think we Kintzels are radicals and upstarts just because we're fighting with the federal inspectors so much. But the way I see it that couldn't be further from the truth. We're not against government at all. We're just for government that makes good sense."

"Do you consider your mine safe?" Kintzel is asked.

"If I didn't I wouldn't be down here," he responds quickly. "No mine is without some risk, but it's the miners that aren't careful that end up having trouble. Not the careful ones. You can't legislate that either. If some fool is determined to take risks, he's going to do it whether you have all these regulations or not. That's the truth.

"You know in 23 years the only accident we've had was a broken thumb Nate got once? That's all. But that doesn't seem to make a difference with the federal government. They don't take our safety record into account. We're lumped in with everybody else, good and bad. To my mind, that doesn't make sense."

When the hoist arrives, we climb in on our stomachs so we can observe the ride to the surface. The hoist seems to alternately claw and stutter to the surface.

Outside the mine again, the sun is blinding and dots form on my eyes, like coming out of a movie theater at mid-day. The air is cold and still. A metallic screech signals the hoist being lowered again as Kintzel and I head toward the shanty. One or two more runs for coal and the brothers will call it a day, he explains. It is a short day by the Kintzels' standards, only a half-shift.

They have decided to break early because it is New Year's Eve. Tomorrow will be a holiday as well. But then the steady cycle that has marked their 23 years on top of Big Lick Mountain will begin again.

"Steady, if nothing else, that's what we are,"Kintzel says as we descend into the make-shift shack. "Steady and just stubborn enough to believe we are right."

DISCUSSION

One of the journalistic aspects of literary journalism that has not been mentioned in detail yet is display of the story. The subject is discussed in chapter 10, but bears mention now because of the way this story was displayed (''packaged'' is the word some editors would use). Perhaps readers of short stories and novels do not pay attention to the typographic elements, but the same cannot be said for newspaper readers. In a newspaper, which is more than just text type, editors make many decisions regarding the packaging of a story. As Roger Fowler (1977) said:

A newspaper article has textual structure in our sense: a disposition of information arranged with headline, sub-headings, paragraphing, capitalization, graphs, photographs. And every text is a discourse, and act of language by an implicit author who has definite design on an identifiable implied reader. (p. 47)

This story appeared in a magazine format. The reader received it as part of the daily *Republican*, but because it was a separate 16-page tabloid-sized package, it could be removed from the daily newspaper and read as desired. Furthermore, the story was accompanied by 18 photographs that did more than illustrate the story; they also helped tell it. In fact, the photographer, Kurt Steidle, received the same billing as Gaul—his name on the cover. The cover was a full-page photograph of the Kintzel brothers.

None of those factors can be overlooked. Fowler (1977) said:

> Different surface structures make a radical difference to the impression the text makes on the reader; to his sense of the author's tone, of the rhythm of the text, of its affiliations with other texts; above all, to the reader's impression of the place of a text and of its author among the thought-patterns of a culture. (p. 11)

Even the headline, its allusion to other works of book-length literary reportage (*Of a Fire on the Moon* by Norman Mailer, for example), is more of a title than a typical newspaper headline (subject-verb-object).

This is the only story in the book that contains the nonjournalistic first person. "Journeys into the far corners of the world, strange adventures, are more exciting when narrated by those who made the trip and saw it all with their own eyes," Leon Surmelian (1968, p. 68) said. This is a story of Gaul's trip. Gaul chose the first person because he envisioned the story being published in a magazine. "For this story to work, I thought it was important for me to play a role. Using the first person freed me to offer my impressions." At the same time, Gaul kept the personal pronoun to a minimum so it did not become intrusive and make the story appear to be about Gaul rather than the Kintzel brothers.

With the first person, Gaul stands in for the reader and represents everyman. The reader can identify with Gaul. Late in the story, for example, he and Harvey Kintzel are riding the hoist on the way out of the mine. Here is Gaul standing in for the reader:

> Miners, I rapidly observed, are a lot like mountain climbers, in an inverted sort of way, relying heavily on a sixth sense of knowing precisely when to shift their weight and use the mountain to their advantage. Kintzel led the way up. Using the same wood rails for support that the hoist rides, he moved quickly and effortlessly ahead. Much faster than a 51-year-old who had suffered a heart attack should be able to, I reasoned. By contrast, I struggled along, probably too cautiously because at several junctions I had to call Kintzel to wait until I caught up to him.

The first person also allows Gaul to help the reader evaluate information. At midpoint in the story, Gaul talks with an official from the federal Mine Safety and Health Administration. Gaul shows the reader Gaul questioning the official, enabling the reader to see Gaul's reporting techniques.

In a way, the use of the first person in this story is reminiscent of *Friendly Fire* by C.D.B. O'Bryan. In that book, O'Bryan traces the quest of one Iowa woman to find out how her son was really killed in Vietnam. She is not satisfied with the explanation that he was a victim of friendly fire—accidental fire from other Americans. At some point late in the book, the mother's refusal to believe the government's version of events forces O'Bryan to conduct his own investigation. The book's point of view shifts from the third person of the mother to the first person of the author. A similar shift occurs in *Fatal Vision* by Joe McGinnis. Gaul limits his first person to impressions and does not draw conclusions the way O'Bryan and McGinnis did, but still there are similarities in the approaches.

Gaul wanted the brothers to tell their own story: "The brothers were home-bred raconteurs and did most of the work for me. All I had to do was organize what they told me and balance some of their assertions with material from MSHA officials."

Gaul, however, gave the story more than journalistic (factual) direction; he also gave the story its literary direction. As noted earlier, the allusory headline is part of the story's literary direction. Gaul also chose a metaphorical beginning—a mountain. "The fact that the brothers were the last independents on Big Lick seemed significant to me, not to mention something of a metaphor for their struggle. The mountain was the foil. From there all I had to do was follow a logical path into the mine."

The story begins with Gaul and Harvey Kintzel going up the mountain to enter the mine. The story ends with the two of them coming out of the mine. The reader has been taken on a journey. The story closes this way:

> "Steady, if nothing else, that's what we are," Kintzel says as we descend into the make-shift shack. "Steady and just stubborn enough to believe we are right."

Gaul picked that direct quotation because he felt it summed up the brothers' dilemma. "I think it is important to end a story with the same kind of impact you look for when you choose a lead," Gaul said. "Often I'll hold a good quote until the end if I'm writing a long piece. A good quote or a well-painted scene can leave a reader thinking about your story after he puts it down." The reader continues to savor the experience much the way he or she might savor a good novel long after the reading is over.

Gaul also relies strongly on description. Look at the opening:

> On a rinsed, cobalt blue morning, Harvey Kintzel and I climbed aboard his 1973 Ford pickup and started up a winding dirt road into the small coal hole he and his three brothers have scraped a living from for the last 23 years.

Gaul emphasizes clear, well-written visual images. "A lot of people have ideas about what a mining area looks like but few people understand the nature of a small operation like the Kintzels. I tried to clear this up by describing their operation in some detail. In general, I tried to blend the brothers words with images that were equally meaningful."

Gaul occasionally uses sentence fragments. To be effective, however, sentence fragments must relate to whole sentences. Sentence fragments are effective as parts of a larger standard grammatical structure. Finally, sentence fragments work best in small doses. Scarcity makes them effective. Abundance diminishes their effectiveness. Here is a paragraph that includes sentence fragments (italicized):

> Today the Kintzels work the same two veins of coal—the Lykens Nos. 6 & 7 veins— they started taking coal from more than 23 years ago. Mining these two veins is a little like trying to squeeze blood from a stone. The pitch is severe, even when one considers that coal rarely lies flat on its side in the anthracite fields. *Thirty-eight degrees. About the same as looking up into the eyes of your dentist.* On top of that, there really isn't all that much coal to speak of, and what is here requires an inordinate amount of work to remove.

Note, too, the use of the analogy with a dentist looking into someone's mouth. The image is universal and will be understood by all readers.

It is worth recalling some of the comments made in chapter 1, especially those about the cyclical nature of life and the originality of vision needed to retell the old stories in new ways. When the retelling occurs, when Gilbert M. Gaul and others like him develop a story in a literary fashion, they are playing on universal themes. In this story, it is the theme of man struggling against elements and other men. The struggle for survival. Gaul does not have to say "this is a story about men struggling for survival." He does it in the way he tells the story.

* * *

Gilbert Gaul wrote again of the Kintzel brothers after joining the staff of the *Inquirer*. In 1986 he wrote an *Inquirer Magazine* piece, a sequel to this article, in which he told of the death of Harvey Kintzel in a mine accident on June 21, 1985. "The large mine disasters always make the news, of course," Gaul wrote, "but death never takes a vacation from the small mines either—a fact Harvey sometimes seemed to conveniently overlook."

Chapter Eight
Roots of Violence

BACKGROUND

Looking around for a major community project to write about and concerned with the crime rate in their hometown, the executive editor and the editor of the editorial page of the *Stockton* (California) *Record* decided to explore the city's crime problem. The result was a five-part series written by Patricia A. Donahue, a general assignment reporter, and Eric P. Best, the editor of the editorial page. Early in developing the series, the various editors involved decided to use case studies packaged with statistics and with commentary from 25 social, legal, business, religious, education, and government leaders. The case studies appeared on one page; the statistics and commentary on a second. "Our hope was to give the reader a mix of approaches and have faith that the 'truth' about crime would reside in the combination of methods for delivering information," Best (1981) said. "The fictionalized tone of the writing, with names changed but otherwise documented from interviews and the public record, was employed to promote greater reader interest and give the reporter more stylistic room in which to capture the sense of the story."

BIOGRAPHIES

Although the story used here was written by Patricia A. Donahue, recognition must also go to Eric P. Best, who wrote two of the five stories in the series in the same style as this one.

Patricia A. Donahue graduated from Ohio State University with a degree in journalism. She worked as a reporter and editorial board member for the university's daily, the *Lantern*. She spent 3 years at other newspapers before going to work for the *Record*.

Eric P. Best graduated from Hamilton College in Clinton, New York, with a degree in English and then worked for 2 years as a reporter for the *Lowell* (Massachusetts) *Sun*. He became a staff writer in the Massachusetts Department of Youth Services before entering Stanford University's masters program in fiction. He then worked as a counselor to delinquent youth in San Francisco (a job he describes as interim) before joining the *Stockton Record* as a political and general assignment reporter. After 4 years of that work, he was made editor of the editorial page and also put in charge of special reporting projects, of which this is one. In 1982 he was chosen as a Nieman Fellow. He subsequently became the economics writer for the San Francisco *Examiner*.

THE STORY

ROOTS OF VIOLENCE
BRUTALITY IN THE HOME:
ABUSED CHILD STRIKES BACK

(Tuesday, July 21, 1981.
© 1981 *The Stockton Record*.)

BY PAT DONAHUE
Of the Record Staff

Larry hit her. And again. Faye fell over the coffee table onto the floor. He grabbed her neck and began choking her, but his grip was weak. The beer had left him unsteady and she broke away.

"Go in there," he shouted, pointing to the bedroom. "And take your clothes off." His words confused her. Sex was the last thing Larry wanted when they fought. She thought perhaps he planned to put her out on the street naked.

She started through the kitchen to the bedroom and caught sight of the claw hammer on the shelf by the sink. She grabbed it and turned. "Larry, don't hit me no more," she said.

Bam! The blow to the side of her head was quick. Stunned momentarily, she raised the hammer in her right hand and backed Larry into the living room, into the arm of the red velour love seat.

"Larry, don't hit me no more," the screamed. He hit her again, this time on her left temple.

The hammer fell. Larry fell. Blood leapt from the left side of his head, onto the yellow curtains, onto the love seat, onto the brown and yellow shag carpet.

The hammer fell four more times. Blood was everywhere. It was a crazy feeling. She sensed the finality to what she was doing, but she didn't stop. Turning the hammer around she hit him four more times, tearing chunks from his neck.

She walked to the kitchen, put the hammer on the counter, just to the right of the sink, and returned to the living room. Then it hit her. She hurried over to Larry, slumped between the love seat arm and the floor. She took his pulse. Dead.

She searched his pockets for the car keys. No, she couldn't run away. They'd find her.

She ran to the neighbors. "I think I've killed Larry," she screamed and ran back to the house. She stood in the living room, staring at Larry, not believing it.

That's where the deputies found her. It wasn't the first time they had come to settle a fight between Larry and Faye.

Faye Burton's troubles with men began a long time before that hot, violent Thursday afternoon in Stockton. When she was four years old, her father moved from the family's two-bedroom San Francisco Bay area flat, leaving Faye's mother to care for her and her two younger brothers. An older brother and sister lived with an aunt. Her father's departure left Faye with just a few memories of him—sleepy mornings when he stopped by her bed with a glass of Kool-aid. A rare spanking that she deserved. Cold, rainy mornings when she'd tiptoe into their room and nestle between him and Momma.

His departure also meant an end, temporarily, to the fights and beatings. Whenever he and her mother got especially drunk, mostly on the weekends, he'd wait until Momma undressed for bed and then whip her with his belt. Faye never knew why.

Life got harder after he left. Momma drank more. Days passed when Faye and her brothers didn't see her at all.

Often Momma told her: "Regardless of what the father does, it is the mother's responsibility to see that the kids get what they need." So Faye began to take on that role.

She didn't really mind the work. The boys weren't bad and she'd whip them like Momma did if they misbehaved. If they were clean and fed and the house was clean when Momma did get home, she wasn't so likely to yell and throw furniture around. She might just go to bed. Things were always better when she woke up.

Those were often the times when Momma pulled Faye and the boys close and rocked them in her arms. Momma worked as hard as she could. She found it difficult to be on her feet all day at the hospital where she worked as a nurses' aide. Faye figured a sickness made her drink so much at night. It had nothing to do with them. Someday, they'd have a new daddy. Things would be better.

And they did get a new daddy. Faye was seven when her mother married Bill, who worked steady and paid the bills. But things weren't better for Faye.

Bill and Momma had lots of fun, drinking and partying. Then the fights started. Bill yelled at Momma. After a while he started shoving her. Eventually he hit her. Momma didn't hit back. Not at first.

Faye would always remember a night when she was 10. She and her brothers could hear yelling in the bedroom. The door flew open and Bill hurried into the living room, Momma on his heels, a butcher knife in her fist. It sliced across his back. The blood spurted. The fight ended.

But the fighting didn't. There were always others, always about the same thing—men. Bill said she wanted others, had been with others. She said she didn't and hadn't. But that didn't stop the fights, which now played to an audience of five children. Momma had two sons with Bill and he treated the four boys the same. He beat them all. Momma spanked the children at times, but Faye least of all. She was an obedient little girl. Bill never spanked her. He said he loved her. He put his arms around her and fondled her. Bill had sex with her almost from the time he moved in until she was 12 years old.

She didn't tell anyone at first. He didn't want her to. Finally she told Momma, who said she didn't believe it. Faye couldn't understand why Momma wouldn't help her, protect her. It was something she would never really understand.

Sex with Bill continued. Faye turned for help to her older brother's wife. Denise told her 12-year-old niece to charge for sex. So she did, sometimes asking and getting $50. Soon after that, Faye's mother began hounding Bill about where his money was going, and his demands on Faye ended. Later, she would demand and get money from other men, too. If she needed money and they wanted sex, it seemed like a fair exchange.

Not all of Faye's childhood was unhappy. She loved school. Most of her grades were As and Bs. She especially liked math. It always made sense—one and one always made two.

In grammar school she met Laurie. They spent hours together on field trips to the city library. Both played violin in the junior high band. Close neighbors in the housing project, they played together after school as well.

And Momma provided happiness, at times.

Despite heavy drinking, she showed up for school activities and applauded loudly when Faye danced or played the violin. She made cupcakes for bake sales and encouraged Faye to learn arts and crafts and go to dances and movies at the Y.

When Faye was 13, in fact, her mother became one of the most popular parents in her daughter's crowd. She allowed the kids to have "a party after the party" at her house. She left the kids alone to drink the liquor and smoke the pot many of them brought.

Faye's partying days ended suddenly. At 14 she was pregnant. It frightened her. But she was also pleased at the prospect of having something of her own that she wouldn't have to share, the way she shared everything with her brothers for so many years. She didn't even tell the baby's father.

But when her mother learned about the pregnancy, she told Faye to find her own place to live. If her daughter was old enough to have her own baby, then she was old enough to take care of it and herself, too.

Faye moved in with a 15-year-old boy she met in school.

From the start, their life was unhappy. Donald punched and kicked her during quarrels that seemed to start over nothing. Jobless and uninterested in school, he loafed. Faye continued high school in special classes for pregnant girls.

Then Matthew was born, and she had to quit school. At 15, she found it hard to concentrate, with a new baby and a job she had found to supplement her welfare checks. When she got pregnant again that year, she decided to have an abortion. She went through it despite her mother's anger. "I know it's not right, but I also know I just can't handle it."

She couldn't handle Donald and the fights any longer, either. Sick of the beatings, she began putting small amounts of toilet bowl cleaner in his breakfast grits, sure he would die over a short period of time. Then she realized that if he died suddenly, she would be the prime suspect. Instead, she took Matthew and left.

There was a period of drifting after that, in and out of school, in and out of relationships with men, many of them much older. She took school where she could find it and watched over Matthew as she had time. At 22, armed with a high school equivalency diploma, she came to Stockton to live with her sister.

It was right after a job interview that Faye met Larry. Waiting for a bus at Main and Stanislaus streets, she was distracted by a blue Gran Torino that pulled up next to her.

A man about 55, thin and sporting a moustache, motioned her to get in. She turned away. He rolled down the window. "I ain't gonna rape you."

"I ain't worried about you raping me," she said. "I can take care of myself."

Within a few weeks of their meeting, Faye moved into Larry's one-story green house in Stockton where he kept cows and chickens. Life seemed pretty good. He fixed breakfast for her, took her shopping, and treated Matthew like the son he never had. His salary from seasonal work and unemployment checks in the off season kept the bills paid.

But there was the drinking, the jealousy and the fights.

Larry drank a lot, mostly beer and mostly on weekends. It brought out the worst. He could turn even the most innocent conversation between Faye and another man into a plot. He accused her of sleeping with every man in Stockton. The accusations were accompanied by beatings. For both of them, it was nothing new.

Larry had seen his own father and mother turn arguments to punching matches. He beat his first wife, Nancy, with his fists, blackening her eyes and knocking out her front teeth. Nancy, who had seen her own mother and father in the same kind of fights, took the beatings for 13 years. Then one day she picked up a pair of scissors and plunged them into Larry's chest. He recovered. The marriage didn't.

It would be much the same with Faye. After a year of living with her, Larry tore his wrist and forearm ligaments in an accident at his job. Use of the arm greatly reduced, he applied for a worker's compensation settlement. Larry began spending his days sitting on the front porch, drinking one beer after another, refusing to let Faye out of his sight. The beer and the jealousy just meant more beatings. She started to fight back.

On a warm spring night, during an argument that began with his drinking, she grabbed a steak knife and slashed Larry's neck and wrist. The knife stopped Larry's fists, but the noise prompted neighbors to call the sheriff's office. Deputies found them drunk, Larry bleeding, and Faye cursing and swinging at them as they entered the house. Larry refused to file charges against Faye. He even refused medical help. There would be more fights before that fatal day in August.

That day would stay with her for some time. She had spent the early morning thinking about her life. How she and Larry spent all of their time together. How it added up to nothing. She and Matthew, 11, watched television. Larry sat on the porch and drank beer.

When Faye's friend, Betty, stopped by and asked Larry if Faye could go back to her place and see her new daughter, he said yes. He even told Faye to enjoy herself.

By the time Faye called him later, though, to ask if Matthew could stay overnight with Betty's son, Larry's mood had changed. In a drunk voice he ordered her home.

Once there, his accusations started again. Faye denied them, as usual. Then he punched her, and she picked up the hammer. The first blow seemed to trigger all the rest, as if each one had been alive in her all along, just waiting to get out.

At 25, Faye had killed a man old enough to be her father.

Almost two years later, Faye sits in the classroom of a California women's prison and talks about her life.

"I deserve this time...if for nothing else but to give me time to think about regrouping."

She is trying to plan her life so she avoids the pitfalls of the past. It will mean less drinking, more working and staying clear of men who try to push her around. It will mean taking fewer things for granted, especially her children.

Drinking is not much of a problem in prison, where liquor is hard to get. Working is something she prepares for each day in nurses' assistant training. Choosing men is something she thinks about a lot.

In the past, she chose men who at first seemed to like her independence, but who later tried to change her.

"I don't allow myself to get pushed around," she says. "If I do, I either get out of that predicament or I take care of it."

With Larry, she didn't get out.

"Yeah, and I took care of it." A split-second later she adds, "I didn't mean to take care of it so finally."

She's sorry about that. She sees no reason for it.

"He died for nothing because what he was saying I did, I didn't do. He said I was out f------ everybody in Stockton, but I never went out on him, not once. He was the only man I never went out on and he accused me of going out on him. It made me sick."

She doesn't dwell on it.

"He's gone and I'm still here and I gotta survive. I was just fed up. That's the feeling I had. I didn't really want to kill him. I had the feeling 'I want to kill you' but I didn't really. When he was dead, I was shocked. I couldn't believe it."

But she admits the idea of such a turn in her life began long ago. "I had a feeling when I was younger I was gonna kill somebody." She was about nine or 10 then. "I had a real bad temper. As I got older, I started taking too much shit, letting it pile up and then acting." She figures she was "acting" out all her anger at Larry when she killed him.

About three months after his death, upon her release on bail from county jail, Faye realized what a difference not having him around made in her life. "I felt—not good that he was dead—but good that I wasn't going to be bothered by him no more. You understand what I'm saying? You can miss somebody and love them, but they're not the best thing for you. I felt like a weight had been lifted off me."

At the same time, however, another weight had been added. She became pregnant a month after her release on bail, by a man she knew years ago. "I was scared. When I got out of jail, I couldn't even enjoy myself. I knew I was going to prison and I couldn't even enjoy myself. I was all uptight."

Her second son, Morris, was born in county jail. Faye left for state prison five days later.

"I want to see him so bad," she says, unsatisfied by photographs her mother sends from Stockton. She feels "cheated."

But she is happy that both boys are with her mother, who, despite the earlier split over Faye's first pregnancy, grew close to her daughter again. Faye is confident her sons will be cared for properly since Momma still adheres to a "spare the rod and spoil the child" philosophy.

One day, while babysitting her son's 2-year-old daughter, Momma whipped the child's legs when she failed to move to the bedroom quickly enough from the living room, where Momma was sipping a pre-lunch beer.

Faye believes that children that age should be punished that way for misbehaving.

Matthew, now 12, doesn't get whippings anymore. He learned to behave properly when he was younger. Faye recalls a time when Matthew went swimming after being forbidden to do so. "I tore his butt up with his belt," she says, adding, "Some parents don't and they don't have control over their kids either."

Faye feels luckier than most at the women's prison. One woman got eight years for killing her husband. Another got 15.

She received two years for voluntary manslaughter—the intentional killing of another in the heat of passion and with provocation—and an additional year for using a weapon. With time credited for county jail and good behavior, she expects to be released in March.

She pleaded guilty to manslaughter, knowing she would receive a prison sentence, rather than go on trial for murder. She didn't think a jury would believe she killed Larry in self-defense. "I didn't think I would beat it."

Could what happened with Larry happen with another man?

Yes, she says. But she plans to avoid it by choosing a man who doesn't beat up women, one who isn't attracted to an independent woman—which she believes she is—with the idea that he can make her dependent.

Still, she isn't sure how much has really changed.

Her words come slowly as she thinks about the man she killed.

"I probably could kill somebody else. The first time was hard.

"The second time—a little easier.

"Probably could put a little more thought into it, too."

DISCUSSION

The authors of the other stories in this book have generally said that the substance of their stories dictated the form, that they had no idea how they were going to write their stories until they analyzed the results of their reporting. This story represents a more conscious effort at deciding form beforehand. The fact that this story is one of five in a series gives added reason for that decision. Continuity had to be maintained.

In selecting the "fictionalized tone," Best not only decided what would go into the story but what would be used separately. The additional material also makes this effort good community-oriented journalism. The statistics and commentary (not reproduced here) provide the reader with answers or solutions on which to act (or not act). Had Best decided to write one story with all of that information under one headline, he could not have preserved the literary approach. The result would have been unwieldy, what with trying to tell Faye's story and intersperse commentary from experts. The literary–expository approach has its merits, but in this story it would have confused the reader because of the many voices and points of view. The literary–expository approach works best with small packages of material (see "A job where nobody complains" in chapter 5) or when a story can be divided into scenes (see "The Suspect" in chapter 4). In this series, the commentary about the crime committed in the literary story is effective because it is presented separately from the literary story.

This treatment reminds me of a point made by Michael Schudson (1978), who described two journalisms in the 1890s—story and information, in which story journalism entertained and interpreted while information journalism provided data (election results, stock market reports, etc.). Best and Donahue have provided both story and information journalism but in a different mix.

Essentially, Donahue divided her story into three parts. She begins with Faye murdering her boyfriend, Larry. Donahue then backs up to present a glimpse of Faye's childhood and early adulthood. This part brings Faye's life up to the murder. The third part occurs 2 years later—in the present—with Faye in prison.

The opening of this story draws the reader in because Donahue is describing something as it happened rather than summarizing what happened. The reader sees the process and will later get to see the probable cause and the apparent effect as Donahue tightly retells the story of Faye. The murder scene was not the original lead in this story. "In my draft," Donahue says, "the murder occurred at the end of the past narrative just before the break to the present." But she changed the lead after a discussion with Best. They both saw three leads in the story, but felt that the murder was the most compelling. There is, of course, something journalistic to beginning a story with an item that is sure to draw in the reader, but any good piece of writing deserves to have a compelling beginning and this story is no exception.

Donahue also uses present–past tense to differentiate between time periods. Says Best, "The tense change you note simply didn't bother me, though I know the rules well enough." The use of the present tense in newspapers is not widely accepted and even the writers in this book disagree on its application to newspaper writing.

One *Record* reporter criticized the series because Best and Donahue did not evaluate and filter the information. To that reporter, the fictionalized approach meant that Best and Donahue were not exercising their gatekeeping functions. Best says:

> I disagree with that since the fictionalized approach requires more careful consideration than traditional news writing. In the latter, you assume that your stricter limits on language and style reduce distortion. In fact, I think straight news writing is often highly distorted because it's a more extreme reduction from events to words. Once you accept that language will distort, then you have to choose what frame of language has the best chance of representing the story. In something as complex as crime, where you don't really know what the causes and effects are, it's a given that you won't capture the "truth." You're trying to paint representatively but impressionistically as well.

Best argues that the writer must select the approach that gets as close to the truth of the story as possible. John Hellmann (1981) said:

> Admirers of conventional journalism have portrayed the conflict with new journalism as one of objectivity versus subjectivity and fact versus fiction. However, it is actually a conflict of a disguised perspective versus an admitted one, and a corporate fiction versus a personal one. . . . Because it is a product of the human mind and language, journalism can never passively mirror the whole of reality, but must actively select, transform, interpret it. (p. 4)

Robert H. Canary and Henry Kozicki (1978) believe that "the pattern of the narrative is itself an interpretative statement" (p. xi).

In this story, one example of interpretation comes in the ending. Donahue could have chosen to emphasize the positive side of the story: Faye's impending release from prison. Instead, Donahue ends with Faye's seemingly calculated statement on killing again. Donahue did not interpret Faye's statement as bravado. "She was serious and her words had a chilling effect on me. I wanted the reader to understand that Faye had had a rough life, had killed somebody, had understood how the criminal justice system had worked in her case and understood what she was saying about future possibilities." Again, a conscious decision determined the ending of this story just as the writer made a decision on the beginning. Her ending brings the story to a conclusion rather than a halt.

John Hellman (1981) contended that the time has come for critics to stop thinking of fictional writing as invention and factual writing as recording and their relationship to each. "Instead," he wrote, "we must speak of different kinds of writing either in terms of their relation to the subject, or in terms of their final direction of meaning, and not try to speak in the one way by reference to the other" (pp. 21-25). Judge the story on intent. Is it an accurate representation of reality? That is the journalistic test it must pass. Writing style has nothing to do with it.

Chapter Nine
The Illegal Odyssey of Don Bernabé Garay

BACKGROUND

John M. Crewdson, a national correspondent for *The New York Times*, received his editor's permission to spend a year writing about immigration in America. In that year (1980), Crewdson wrote more than 40 stories on the smuggling of humans across the Mexican border, the travels of Cuban refugees, on migrant camps, border jails, Chicago sweatshops, and corruption among United States immigration authorities. The stories spurred an investigation and policy review by the Justice Department. Even before Crewdson began the series, he had made friends in the Arizona Farmworkers Union who vouched for him when he was looking for illegal aliens to write about. He met the subject of this story that way. This particular story took Crewdson 3 weeks, which included reporting, solving logistical problems, and waiting for the aliens to assemble. For the entire series, Crewdson won a Pulitzer Prize for national reporting.

BIOGRAPHY

John M. Crewdson graduated with a bachelor's degree in economics from the University of California at Berkeley and then did graduate study in politics, philosophy, and economics at Oxford University in England. Between his undergraduate and graduate studies he worked for 1 year as an intern for the *Times* in New York City and Washington, DC. When he returned from Oxford, he joined the *Times* as a staff reporter in Washington, a position he held for 5 years before becoming a national correspondent. Eventually he became a reporter in the *Chicago Tribune's* Los Angeles bureau.

THE STORY

The Illegal Odyssey of Don Bernabé Garay

(Sunday, December 14, 1980).
© 1980 by the New York Times Company.
Reprinted by permission.)

By JOHN M. CREWDSON
Special to The New York Times

WHY, Ariz. — It was the sweetest and gentlest of desert evenings, pitch-black except for a sliver of new moon and the light from a hundred thousand stars. Nearby, a coyote scampered among the stately organ pipe cactuses, its occasional mournful howl slicing the silence like a jagged knife.

Presently the stillness was broken by a softer sound, a brief, two-toned whistle. For half a minute there was nothing, then an identical whistle was heard from beyond the rise, followed by a flash of light and an answering flash, the signal that the way was clear. Within seconds, shadowy figures emerged from the desert. Smiling and talking softly, they gathered in a circle near the little-used highway.

After a moment, Bernabé Garay stepped forward. A dignified, cheerful man with a fondness for battered hats, "Don Berna" had led the others here: by bus, third class, from their cloud-high, stone-poor village in the Sierra Madre; by pickup truck, at danger rates, from the border town of Sonoita to the gap in the barbed wire where, a few hours earlier, at nightfall, they had become illegal aliens; on foot, pressing hard, wary of rattlesnakes and border patrols, to a prearranged pickup point here in the Arizona desert. As it would prove, they had yet to face the greatest obstacles in their journey in search of work in the citrus groves around Phoenix.

Driven North by Poverty

Like uncounted millions of their countrymen before them, like the millions who will follow their well-worn path, they were driven north by the astounding poverty of rural Mexico, where life reduces to the simplest of equations: work or starve. But there was no work for them in Mexico, and so they were here.

As it was, they were among the last men to leave the village for America. The only ones left there now, Don Berna said, "are those that are older than me." Despite his 55 years, Bernabé set the others a rapid pace. They covered the 20 miles from the border in four hours, but they are mountain men from the Mexican village of Ahuacatlán, and for them such a walk is a brisk stroll.

The first leg of their journey was remarkable only for its monotony. As in years past, the 60 men of Ahuacatlán traveled for two days and nights by third-class bus to the Mexican border town of Sonoita, a favored jumping-off place for those seeking to enter the United States illegally. They expected no problems, but this year the crossing proved more nettlesome than usual.

It was near here that 13 from El Salvador died last July, abandoned without water by some of their Mexican guides, unfamiliar with the unforgiving ways of the desert. The discovery of their dehydrated bodies caused some embarrassment to the immigration authorities in Mexico, who are now cracking down on illegal border crossers.

The men of Ahuacatlán are old hands at such crossings—Don Berna has been coming to the United States to work for nearly three decades—and they know enough to walk through the desert in the cool of the evening. It was in finding someone to take them to the crossing point that they encountered the problem.

That Monday afternoon, Don Berna, two of his sons and four other men, wearing the straw cowboy hats favored by workers from Mexico, gathered under a bridge over a sluggish creek in Sonoita to plan their route. In a dusty gully littered with red and silver Tecate beer cans, the men huddled over maps, marking the spot 30 miles east of town to which José, a man with a truck, had promised to take them for $7 apiece.

Despite his age, Bernabé climbed the creek bank like a mountain goat, walked to a nearby pay telephone and placed a call to a number in Phoenix. The voice on the other end assured him that transportation would be waiting at the pickup point in the Papago Indian Reservation.

But when Bernabé returned, José the driver announced his reluctance to make the trip. Anyone caught driving workers into the desert these days was sure to get in trouble, José said, although for $600 he might consider taking the risk. Another conference was held, but the answer was no. "The workers feel that it is too much money," said Bernabé.

As it grew dark, about half of the group, eager to reach Phoenix, decided to set off along the border on foot. But Bernabé and the others, sensing some kind of danger, elected to stay behind in Sonoita. José, ever accommodating, sold them tacos filled with beans and a Mexican sausage called chorizo that his wife had prepared for just such an eventuality. The men scouted the area for cardboard boxes to use for mattresses and carried them into the arroyo above the creek.

Agent on Aliens' Trail

It was not until later that Bernabé and his friends learned how lucky they were. A Border Patrol agent from the tiny station here at Why, riding his horse at dusk, found the tracks left by the splinter group as they came across the border. For six hours the Mexicans walked, the agent hard on their trail. Shortly after midnight, they reached the ranch of a Papago Indian named David, who they hoped could arrange rides to Phoenix for them. But they were met instead by other Border Patrol agents, including one in an airplane.

While their fellow villagers spent Monday night in the Gila Bend jail, Bernabé and the others slept soundly on the ground in Sonoita, and when they awoke the next morning they went again to visit José. They had decided, they told him, to pay his price.

Most of Tuesday, Bernabé and the others languished in Sonoita, telling stories and waiting for dark. At noon they bought some chicken from a restaurant for $4 a plateful, an exorbitant price. The chicken, Bernabé said, was "terrible." But the merchants in Mexican border towns like Sonoita know that those who come to cross the border are a long way from home, and take advantage of them accordingly.

At 4:30 P.M., José arrived with his truck, collected his money and drove the men to a desolate spot east of Sonoita where crossing the border is as easy as crossing the street. There is almost no border there at all, just a barbed-wire fence strung between red metal poles, its twisted strands filled with holes large enough for a man to climb through.

By 5:30, the group was walking north. There are only five Border Patrol agents assigned to this 3,300-square-mile stretch of desert, and mass arrests like the one at David's ranch are not an everyday occurrence. The real danger is from the rattlesnakes that come out to bask in the cool of the desert night. Stepping on one means being bitten, and those who pass through this country tell of the skeletons they see along the way.

Sorry to Leave Home

The men were traveling very light. Bernabé carried with him only a gallon jug of water and a sack containing two spare shirts and two pairs of trousers.

"We walked very, very fast," Bernabé said later. "We pushed it very hard." They saw no sign of the Border Patrol and only three snakes, which they killed with sticks.

It was 9:30 when they reached the pickup point, a large sand dune just off Arizona 1, which leads directly to the border. The moon had set an hour earlier, but the sky was filled, as someone said, with "cinquente" stars, literally 50 but figuratively "countless." For men from a poor village like Ahuacatlán, 50 of anything—50 cows, 50 shirts, 50 acres of land—is an unimaginable number.

As he stood with the others waiting for a ride, Bernabé spoke about the village he would not see again until the citrus harvest ended next July, and about Pilar, his wife, and the five children he had left behind. He was very sorry not to be home, he said, "but this is the only way I can make money."

$100 for Drive to Phoenix

Just then, bouncing across the desert in a rattletrap blue Pontiac, there came a welcome sight, a smiling, 18-year-old alien smuggler named Ricardo, wearing the black leather jacket that is the unofficial badge of his profession. Ricardo—at least that was the name he was using that night—is himself an illegal alien, "from Sinaloa," he said proudly, the Mexican state with a reputation for producing fast operators.

For $100 apiece, Ricardo was to drive the men to Phoenix, seven at a time, two trips that night and two the next. For two days' work, he stood to clear nearly $3,000, the kind of money that has made alien smuggling a booming business. At those prices, Ricardo could afford a much better car. But he developed a taste for junk heaps last year, after the Border Patrol began impounding vehicles used to transport illegal aliens.

His profits are high, but Ricardo also has a lot of idle time. He was here most of the previous night, for example, waiting for the men who had decided to stay in Sonoita. It was just as well. An undercover Customs agent, wearing an outlandish cowboy costume, had been cruising up and down the back roads, stopping and searching every car in sight.

But this Tuesday night, the agent was nowhere to be seen. Bernabé, his three sons and four others piled into Ricardo's car, and Ricardo sped off toward Phoenix, his taillights glowing red against the blackness of the rugged mountains.

•

Since its founding in the late 16th century, Ahuacatlán has endured 400 years of solitude without complaint. Hidden away in the blue-green Sierra Madre, it is reached by a narrow, twisting roller coaster of a road, high enough in some places that travelers can reach out and touch the clouds. So isolated, so inconsequential a place is it that residents of San Juan del Rio, 100 miles to the south, have never heard its name. But then, Ahuacatlán has known more departures then arrivals.

Seen from a distance, its pastel houses dripping color against the mountainside, it might be mistaken for Shangri-la. Up close, such a mistake is not possible. Few of the houses have electricity, none have plumbing and some are barely standing beneath their thatched roofs. A handful of ill-stocked shops face the plaza where women, their faces hidden behind bright shawls, slowly pass with baskets tottering on their heads. What is there to hurry for in Ahuacatlán?

Like hundreds of villages across central Mexico, Ahuacatlán these days is only half a place, a village without fathers or husbands. A thousand people—the women and children, the old and the idle—live there now and perhaps another thousand, all men, are in the United States.

"I call my parish a widow's parish," Padre Tomás Caño, the earnest, handsome young village priest, said with a sigh as he sat in the rectory of his crumbling church. "Most of the wives are alone here with their children. This is a very big problem for them, the family disintegration."

"The men don't want to work in the fields here. The harvest, it is very bad, and people are so poor that they need money quickly, in order to eat."

And so, each autumn, the men go north, and each summer they return, bringing dresses and gifts and, always, money from America. So closely is Ahuacatlán bound to the American economy that the preferred medium of exchange here is not the peso but the dollar.

Summers are a happy time in Ahuacatlán. "But when the money is finished," Father Tomás went on, "the men say, 'Let's go again,' and then the women are not so happy. They come to me and say, 'I have no money, no food, my husband is not here, I don't know what to do.' " Shopkeepers extend credit, and money may be sent home from the United States, but the mails are not reliable and eventually the credit runs out. The winters in Ahuacatlán are long and cold.

When the men come home, they speak of their time in America as a great adventure. But the priest, who hears their confessions, knows the truth. "Up there," he said, "the problems are very terrible for them." But except for the men without families to feed, America is the only choice.

Ahuacatlán means "land of avocados," and its residents agree that avocado trees must have covered these lush hillsides once. But the avocados grow here no longer, and neither does much else. Like Bernabé Garay, many of the men of Ahuacatlán own a few acres of steep mountain land and in the summertime they try to grow some corn and beans. "A lot of work for no money," is what Bernabé says.

Each summer, fewer men return to Ahuacatlán then left the year before, and it is always to Father Tomás that their wives bring the official telegrams for translation. "They have an accident in the fields," he said, "or by the knife, or by the gun." Or there is no word at all: "They go and we know nothing about them. Their wives go to the authorities, nothing. Some of these women, they want to marry again, but they cannot." There is no divorce in Ahuacatlán.

Bass Drum, Church Bells

The village is a patriarchy without patriarchs, and it has not learned to cope with the stresses that brings. The children are growing up without fathers, and each year they seem more restless. "Now they want to go to *dances*," said Father Tomás, arching his eyebrows as if to ask, "What next?" There are no fathers to tell them no. Ahuacatlán has a school but the children do not want to study hard. "They dream only to go to the United States," Father Tomás said, "to have a good adventure and have money."

Nearly everyone over 25 in Ahuacatlán is illiterate, and most residents of all ages are in poor health. "When the kids are born they are not very healthy in their minds," the priest said, "retarded. Their health is very poor." Malnutrition is one reason, but some from Ahuacatlán have learned that they have been exposed, in the lemon groves of Arizona, to a toxic and now illegal pesticide known as DBCP that can affect human reproduction.

Despite the stunning natural beauty, a visitor to Ahuacatlán cannot help wondering why the people cling to its misery. The answer seems to be that the village is all they know. "They think they are safe here, morally speaking."

As twilight came to the village, a man appeared in the plaza with a bass drum and beat it loudly to announce that the cantina was open. Muttering, Father Tomás pulled on his white cassock and hurried off to answer with a peal of church bells for evening mass. "My people drink too much beer," he said.

•

The cock crows early in Ahuacatlán, and though it was not yet dawn Pilar Garay had been up for some time, laying a wood fire beneath the grate in her sparse kitchen. Its fragrant pine smoke mingled with that of a hundred other fires as, across the village, water began to boil for porridge and coffee. The Garays' adobe house, which Bernabé built himself a quarter century ago, has electricity. But water for cooking and washing is still hauled up from the river, as it has been for hundreds of years.

Promptly at 8 o'clock Primitivo Perez, an elderly neighbor, dropped by for his morning ration of Pilar's coffee. Lest anyone think him lazy, Mr. Perez explained that he was retired; like nearly all the old men, most of his working life was spent in the United States.

In another corner of the kitchen, near an ancient, pedal-driven sewing machine, sat 15-year-old Rafael Garay. Rafael had finished the sixth grade, all that the village school has to offer, and now he was biding his time, waiting to join his father and older brothers in the Arizona citrus groves. He was ready to go now, he said, and his eagerness made Pilar smile. Perhaps, she replied, next year.

Rafael is the same age as the two sons of Onorio Garcia, who owns what passes for a hardware store in the plaza. Mr. Garcia's sons also dream of going to America, but as students. They are attending an expensive private academy in San Luis Potosi, several miles away. One hopes to be a doctor, the other an architect, and Mr. Garcia, who has a battered yellow truck and a wristwatch, is one of the few in Ahuacatlán who has the money to help his sons realize their dreams. Despite his education, Rafael Garay, for example, knows that the only way he will get to America is as a farmhand.

With a husband and three sons working in America, Pilar said, she hoped she would be able to make ends meet. In the old days, Bernabé alone might manage to save only $50 in an entire harvest. With the beginnings of unionization in the Arizona citrus industry, wages have improved, and last season he sent home $1,200. This year, with Reginaldo, 28, Kiko, 23, and 18-year-old Bernabé Jr. working too, they may save as much as $6,000, but nearly a quarter of that must be set aside for next year's journey.

Is she sad that her husband and sons will not be home for Christmas? "Si," Pilar said, "muy triste." But Bernabé has not been home for the last 29 Christmases, ex-

cept for 1976, when he fell off a ladder in the groves, broke three ribs and came to
Ahuacatlán to recuperate.

•

It was just north of Ajo, Ariz., that Ricardo the smuggler ran out of gas. As his
car rolled to a stop, Bernabé and the other passengers burst out and scrambled up the
hill to hide in the brush at the side of the highway. The men watched a policeman arrive, they watched as he spoke over his radio, and they watched the Border Patrol
cruiser drive up and take Ricardo away. All night they stayed in the bushes, and they
were very quiet.

At dawn Kiko Garay made his way carefully down from the hillside and found a
telephone. One call to the efficient underground smuggling network, and another ride
was on the way.

Ricardo was permitted, as are most illegal aliens, to return to Mexico "voluntari-
ly," a practice that saves the Immigration and Naturalization Service much time and
money. Had he been caught with Bernabé and the others, he almost certainly would
have spent a minimum of six months in jail for alien smuggling. But this arrest was
a minor inconvenience. The next day Ricardo was back in Phoenix and back in business.

When Bernabé and the others reached Phoenix on Wednesday they went to the ranch
where they worked last year. The lemons were not yet ready for picking, so they spent
that day, and the next, setting up housekeeping, renewing old friendships and playing
cards.

It was not until Thursday night, as the desert air began to chill, that Bernabé remembered the blankets that he left the summer before with his friend, Manuel Diaz. He
resolved to get them in the morning.

In past years, the Border Patrol raided the citrus ranches every so often, picking
up the workers and sending them back to Mexico. But this year, because of manpower
shortages and new regulations, such raids have been very few. Once they reach the
ranches the workers are virtually safe from arrest. It is when they venture out that
they court danger.

And so it was early that Friday morning, when Bernabé and Kiko went round to
Manuel Diaz's house to retrieve the blankets. He was not at home, and as they walked
away from his house a lime-green Border Patrol van screeched to a halt in front of
them. It was at that point that Don Bernabé Garay, father of nine, a man of respect
and influence in Ahuacatlán, secretary general of the struggling Arizona Farmworkers
Union, became a statistic.

The next hours were unpleasant ones. Bernabé and Kiko were taken first by the
Border Patrol to the station in Phoenix, then to a holding cell in Tucson. At 9 that
night they were driven to Nogales, Mexico, and let go.

A week after leaving Ahuacatlán, Bernabé was back in Mexico. On Sunday morning, he and Kiko took the bus to Sonoita and set out again in search of José the driver.
They finally found him and struck another deal, for $30 apiece, and on Sunday the
two men retraced their steps along the border, through the desert and back to Phoenix.
Nine days after leaving home, $300 poorer and without having earned a penny to send
to Pilar, Bernabé returned to the ranch.

At 8 o'clock Monday morning, Bernabé finally went to work. He worked furiously
all day, hauling his heavy canvas bag up and down the stepladders propped against
the tall lemon trees. By 5:30, he had filled his bag 82 times and picked 3,690 pounds

of lemons, an impressive total for a man half his age. He was paid $41, slightly over a penny a pound but far more money than he could have earned in Mexico a week, if he could have found a job there. Bernabé Garay was a happy man at last.

DISCUSSION

This story fits into the category of "slice of life" in which a writer focuses on one person and one event in that person's life. It is a short story. It qualifies as a short story, to quote the definition of short story from *A Dictionary of Literary, Dramatic, and Cinematic Terms* (Barnet, Berman, & Burto, 1971) because it "focuses on a single character in a single episode, and, rather than tracing his development, reveals him at a particular moment" (pp. 100-101). Thus, Bernabé's growth as a character is not traced; in fact, the reader is confined to this one incident only and is left to fill in the past and the future. That seemingly limited aspect of this story does not detract from it. That is its strength—it has a narrow focus.

Some might consider Crewdson's lead description for description's sake and question its relevance to the rest of the story. But they would be wrong. First, the lead sets the mood for the reader and establishes the nature of the story. After all, this is a story about illegal aliens—people who for the most part enter the United States under cover of darkness. The lead also establishes the environmental conditions under which the action is taking place. It has another practical function. "I began the story with the desert scene," Crewdson says, "because I thought it was dramatic; also because it represented the entry of Bernabé and the others into the country and that's really what I was writing about—illegal immigration."

The vivid detail of the lead continues throughout the story. For example, early in the story Crewdson writes:

> That Monday afternoon, Don Berna, two of his sons and four other men, wearing the straw cowboy hats favored by workers from Mexico, gathered under a bridge over a sluggish creek in Sonoita to plan their route. In a dusty gully littered with red and silver Tecate beer cans, the men huddle over maps, marking the spot 30 miles east of town to which Jose, a man with a truck had promised to take them for $7 apiece.

The detail—right down to the brand name on the beer can—puts the reader under the bridge over a sluggish creek in a dusty gully littered with red and silver Tecate beer cans. Crewdson could have just said that the seven met to plan their trip. Instead, he provides the scene for the reader. The reader can see the meeting as it takes place. The reader is present for the discussion.

The story ends nicely too. Crewdson packs much information into the last paragraph, covering 9½ hours of work in five sentences and closing with Bernabé's state of mind. At last, the goal of the man introduced in the beginning is revealed to the reader. Crewdson ties the story together with the final paragraph.

State of mind in literary features raises questions about whether a story is journalism. State of mind is unverifiable. In this book, wherever state of mind appears, it is because the reporter asked the character in the story or because the character volunteered the information. In this story, Bernabé told Crewdson he was happy. It made for a nice ending, but it also points up the need for thorough reporting that must precede an effort like this. Crewdson spent nearly 3 weeks on this story and traveled to Mexico, which he had not originally intended to do until "I realized that I had to see what Bernabé was *leaving* in addition to where he was going." The reporter in Crewdson fed the writer in Crewdson.

As for the writing, Crewdson sounds like others in this book. "The story wrote itself," he says. "I had been composing in my head as we went along and by the time I sat down to write I had a good idea of just what I wanted to say. It all came out rather easily." Writing and polishing took 2 days. Crewdson says that the organization of the story came more easily to him than a more formal news story because he followed the chronology of his reporting. Chronology provides a good overall direction in which to take a story.

In effect, the story contains three scenes and one exposition. The first scene opens with the aliens crossing the border at Why, Arizona. Only after Crewdson joined the group did he realize that he had to visit the town in Mexico that they had left. So he went there. That trip generates exposition on the town followed by scene 2, which introduces the reader to Don Bernabé's wife. The final scene returns the reader to the United States, to Don Bernabé, and to his work.

Also worth noting is the headline, which is more of a title than a traditional headline. Crewdson slugged the story "Odyssey," and, as he says, "that helped set the tone." The headline writer picked up on the slug. Crewdson says "the national copy desk at the *Times* has some of the best headline writers around." That is good, for research suggests that the headline sets the tone for a story and deserves as much attention as the other aspects in the editing process. A good story deserves a good headline. The headline/title discussed here helps establish Crewdson's piece as a short story.

Chapter Ten
Review and Emphasis

ISSUES—AND SOME ANSWERS

One of the major issues in literary feature is the problem of writers who stress style over substance. As Walker Gibson (1966) said, "One appreciates any effort by journalists to make the reading of the news less of a chore and a bore. Nobody wants to be dull. But if the alternative to dullness is dishonesty, it may be better to be dull" (p. 54).

In 1981, a reporter for *The Washington Post* admitted that a story bearing her byline and the just-announced winner of the Pulitzer Prize for feature writing had been fabricated by her. The Pulitzer committee immediately gave the prize to a reporter for *The Village Voice*, and it seemed that the tragedy for Janet Cooke and the good fortune for Teresa Carpenter would end there.

But it did not. Soon people came forward to complain about one of Carpenter's stories, basing some of their objections on an unattributed sentence that suggested Carpenter had interviewed someone in prison when admittedly she had not. At the same time a columnist for *The New York Daily News* resigned after a British newspaper challenged the substance of one of his columns and after he admitted using a false name for one of the people he wrote about. On the other side of the American continent, a reporter for the Associated Press resigned after admitting that an article she had written about a 200-mile-an-hour ride down a California freeway was actually based on several brief rides and on interviews with several drivers, not just one. Additionally, portions of her article were virtually the same as an article in *New West* magazine.

If anything can give journalism a bad name in general and literary feature writing in particular, it is the misuse and abuse of literary techniques to make stories

95

sound better than they really are. In a report on the tainted Pulitzer Prize mentioned earlier, the National News Council (1981) said:

> The dangers on that count have been heightened in recent years by a variety of developments that have caused many newspapers to move more and more toward magazine-model brightness in writing style and further and further from their traditional emphasis on hard news rooted in factuality. (p. 48)

Nothing there disputes the technique, just condemns the abuse of the technique. The abuses include composites and compressions. If the literary feature writer discovers a hole that cannot be filled honestly, the writer should admit it rather than make something up. Remember Gibson (1966): "It may be better to be dull" (p. 54). On the other hand, writers need to realize the truth in a comment by Barry Lopez (1984): "Lying is the opposite of story" (p. 52).

Given other newspaper practices, however, the News Council's criticism about the writing style is fatuous. For years, newspapers have used black and white line drawings to illustrate stories and no one has given second thought that these drawings are fabrications. Cooke's story was accompanied by drawings that were based on her reporting. The artist who made the illustrations did not see the 8-year-old "shooting up," yet that is what the illustrations show. If the answer to the question is that the illustrations were only for effect, then the next question is: At what point does effect end and reality begin?

And what is reality? Journalists would claim that objectivity breeds reality. Even that creed is questionable. "There is no way of observing neutral facts neutrally," John M. Ellis (1974) wrote. "We must decide where to look and how to abstract from what we find, and both these decisions are results of the vantage point from which we begin" (pp. 193–94). Most journalists would accept that, admitting then that they try to present all facts in an issue and that is as close to reality as they come. But in literary feature writing, which allows the reader to get facts from the people in the story "unfiltered" by one reporter, is not reality approximated better (if one can approximate reality in degrees)? The stories herein suggest an affirmative answer.

For the journalist writing literary features the answer lies in good reporting. In a working draft of a policy statement on ethical considerations, the *Boston Globe* (National News Council, 1981) said:

> Reconstruction of events is a valuable journalistic tool. The *Globe* should be extremely careful in putting such narratives together. The material should be based on reporting. Someone present, preferably more than one person and preferably a participant, should have notes or a clear memory of exactly what happened and exactly who said what. (p. 136)

Pat Donahue used public records wherever she could to reconstruct the life of

Faye. At one point in the story, Donahue wrote: "Not all of Faye's childhood was unhappy. She loved school. Most of her grades were As and Bs. She especially liked math. It always made sense—one and one always made two." To write that Donahue checked court records and interviewed Faye and her mother separately (Faye and her mother did not talk to each other between interviews, Donahue says). Additionally, Donahue attempted to check school records, but Faye's grammar school had been torn down and her records were not available. The lesson is: One source is usually not enough for the literary feature writer reconstructing events. The good reporter documents and confirms all information.

What of attribution tags? They can get in the way of a literary stylist, yet the lack of attribution tags identifying sources of information strikes at the essence of good journalism. By the same token, a proliferation of anonymous or unidentified sources has not made editors uncomfortable enough to stop the practice. Viewed in the tradition of anonymous sources, the unattributed reconstruction should not bother editors that much. Still, the absence raises a question: Is a story less journalistic because the reader does not know the source of each piece of information? After all, journalists publish the names of sources not only to protect themselves (if attributed information is incorrect or false) but also to enable the reader to evaluate information based on each reader's perception of the source.

In the Teresa Carpenter story that caused complaints is this line: "Now, from his cell at Rikers Island, Sweeney denies that they ever had a relationship." Later, she wrote: "Sweeney was flattered, but could not help feeling that Lowenstein was being ironic." And later: "Sweeney began to believe his mind was being read." As it turns out, Carpenter never interviewed Sweeney, but the reader is not told that in the story. None of that means the preceding information is wrong, but it does raise the question about technique. Does a literary approach put more strain on the reporter and on the newspaper's credibility? Unsourced information leaves a gap through which a dishonest reporter intent on drama or effect can weasel false information. Again, the obligation falls to editors to raise doubts and check information.

Does not the lack of attributed sources place the literary feature writer at the mercy of sources? If a source knows that the information he is about to provide will appear unattributed, what is going to stop the source from giving inaccurate or self-serving information? The idea is not as far-fetched as it may seem, given that hard-news journalists are dependent on sources, some of whom request anonymity for no other reason than self-interest. The question is not raised to suggest that literary feature writing needs line-by-line attribution, but to show that the practice of not always identifying sources already exists in more typical journalistic writing. Dismissing literary feature writing because it uses anonymous or unnamed sources begs the larger question.

The questions do not come with quick and easy answers, although some suggestions do exist. One reason the writer of a literary feature might not use sources throughout is that the continued repetition gets in the way of style. Can a list of sources appear before or after the story? Would footnotes satisfy the curious and the stylist? What about modified footnotes? In his essay "The Selection of Reality," Edward Jay Epstein (Abel, 1981) said:

> If news media clearly and honestly stated the constraints under which they operate, the adjustment would be far easier to make. Unfortunately, they tend to hide rather than explain these constraints. . . . The value of news to the public would be greatly enhanced if news organizations revealed, rather than obscured, the methods by which they select and process reality. (p. 132)

The *Boston Globe* (National News Council, 1981, p. 136) policy cited earlier also contains this statement:

> We should tell our readers clearly and early that the story is pieced together from interviews, documents, notes and whatever. In addition, from time to time the story should remind readers of the basis for our material and the possible bias of the source. (p. 136)

The *Stockton Record* series includes this comment in the upper left-hand corner of each day's opening page: "Based on more than 100 interviews and review of public documents, these stories emerged to show the major forces behind Stockton's crime rate. Names have been changed to protect the privacy of the individuals involved."

Another approach allows a writer to begin literarily but after establishing the story line calls for phrasing such as this from a Sunday newspaper magazine article: "The Cone burglary—reconstructed here from interviews and trial transcripts—was just one in a long string of break-ins that plagued affluent North Carolina neighborhoods in 1974." Whatever method is used, literary features will have no credibility with editors or readers if they lack some form of source identity or a way of externally checking the information in the story. Some of the problems discussed go unresolved; solutions to others appear later.

THE PRACTICAL

What type of story lends itself to literary treatment? Should the entire newspaper read like a collection of short stories? Is the inverted pyramid to be turned on its base?

When it comes to story types, literary feature writers can draw on many events to write literary features. Look at the stories in this book. Crime provides much material, but only when it can be documented and events can be filled in with interviews and double checking. Because of its documentation, a trial might lend itself to literary treatment, especially on those days when the victim or a witness is telling what happened. Early in the story, however, the readers must be told that they are reading an account of testimony, not a proven account of the crime. In general, any event a reporter can verify or observe in progress (smuggling of aliens, digging of graves, burying of a narcotics investigator) can provide the substance to be placed on a literary framework. Remember: The story cannot succeed if it does not focus on people rather than events.

Whatever the event, the reporting effort must be herculean. A good writer is not enough for a literary feature. "Pity the stylist without a story, lost in the mires of self-expression," said Leon Surmelian (1968, p. 237). "The style cannot replace the action, nor the action replace the style" (p. 237). Roy Peter Clark (1980), who went from teaching college English to working as a reporter and is now a writing coach, says: "My greatest lesson as a journalist, and I have incorporated it into my teaching, is the importance of reporting. Without it, there is no good writing" (p. xiv). One newspaper feature writer can even put a figure on how much reporting has to be done. "You have to know five times as much as you're ever going to use in the story," says Cynthia Gorney (Clark, 1980, p. 63) of *The Washington Post*. (Reading that, a former Washington reporter turned journalism professor and journalism ethicist put the figure at 10.)

The amount of time the journalists in this book spent reporting in their stories varies from 1 day to 1 year (3 if you count time spent acquiring background knowledge). Richard Ben Cramer, who estimates his reporting time on the Sadat funeral at 20 hours, points out that he had been in Egypt many times before the funeral and had written stories about Sadat and Egypt. "You can't put a time on that," he says. Doris Wolf's funeral story was preceded by related work on the dead police officer's life, and she had read other stories about him before attending his funeral. "I had an idea of what kind of man he was," she says, "and therefore what kind of man filled that job."

The team reporting effort reflected in Donald C. Drake's story is not without precedent. Major news events often require the reporting skills of many people and centralized writing by one. The reporting time for the Drake-written story was 48 hours.

Mike Sager's reporting time included one day in which he attended a cattle sale and talked to several farmers, the mayor, some townspeople, and the county extension agent, who set up his visit to the Smith farm, where he spent an entire day reporting. John M. Crewdson's 3 three weeks included waiting for something to happen, time that cannot be discounted in any literary feature enterprise.

Finally, Gilbert M. Gaul's reporting gets a mention not only for the length of time (1 year) but also because he applied a seldom-used reporting method—suing for information under the federal Freedom of Information Act. Again, all good reporting requires documentation.

Format plays a minor role in literary feature writing. Newspapers have become increasingly interested in how they look, and efforts have been made to package the news. The two best examples of packaging can be found in Gaul's 16-page tabloid and the *Stockton Record*'s 2-page presentation with the literary approach on one page and statistics and expert commentary on the other. Doris Wolf's story appeared on a section front with related photographs; other series received more routine handling, although they were in some way set off from the rest of the news.

The story on illegal aliens appeared under a three-column photograph and headline in the bottom-left quadrant of page 1, which is not cause for comment in most newspapers, but for *The New York Times*, which has been stingy with packaging in its news sections, the display was extraordinary. Crewdson was pleased with the way the story was headlined ("The Illegal Odyssey of Don Bernabé Garay") and laid out. "I thought the pictures, and the way they were laid out, were extremely dramatic and effective," Crewdson says, even though about 500 words were cut from the story so the continuation could be contained on one page with photographs. Packaging, of course, will not make a story a literary feature, but packaging can help establish the story's specialness for the reader.

THE TECHNIQUE

No single sentence will ever reveal the whole of good writing; good writing is something that resides as much in the attitude of the writer as it does in the technique. Ben Jonson said in 1640 that the best writers of his time "imposed upon themselves care and industry; they did nothing rashly; they obtained first to write well, and then custom made it easy and a habit." A literary feature writer is a habitually good writer and is also someone who has thought about writing. Talk to reporters honored for their writing and they will reveal how carefully they thought out a particular story (even if they first say: "Oh, the story wrote itself.")

For Donald C. Drake, the approach was that of a playwright or filmmaker. He plotted the story in that he knew what each "scene" was going to be about and how it would fit into the overall story. Max Hall (Lyons, 1965) of the Associated Press wrote approvingly of the tension-resolution approach.

> Suppose a baseball game is broken up by a home run in the ninth inning. The writer reports that fact in his lead—the top-heavy treatment. But somewhere in the body of the story, he makes a detailed narrative out of the events in the ninth inning leading up to the climax. And if he handles it well, there is a certain suspense about it. It is not the "whodunit" kind of suspense which would exist if the reader were in the dark as to the outcome. It is the kind of suspense that has been aptly called "waiting for the expected." (pp. 290–291)

Hall made his suggestion in 1950. More recently, Roy Peter Clark of the Poynter Institute for Media Studies has advocated a similar approach, which he called the "hourglass" (Clark, 1984).

Mike Sager feels the pressure of a standard format that includes a "so-what [para]graph, which tells the readers exactly why the story was written." Others call such a paragraph the "nut graph," and editors complain loudly when it is not high enough in the story. "Ideally," Sager says, "this graph says something like 'Joe Smith is one of . . .' Then, more quotes, another graph, more quotes. And so on." Sager admits that the so-what graph helps the reader by telling immediately what the story is going to say. "They can read the third graph and decide if they are interested.'' But Sager has another standard. ''I consider my time wasted if my story is dismissed out of hand on the basis of subject. How do the readers know they're not interested if they haven't read the story? Life is fascinating, and if told properly, any slice of it can be too.'' For Sager, then, each story produces its own form and any attempt to write one story like another is unfair to the writer and the reader.

Good organization guides the flow of any story. For Tom Oliphant, who wrote a series of stories on a blizzard in 1978 for the *Boston Globe*, the narrative approach is a good one to use in reconstructing major events (Clark, 1979, p. 118). Several stories in this book attest to the strength and order the narrative approach can bring to a story.

Skillful organization usually shows in the work of a writer who thinks first about the job ahead. Richard Zahler (Clark, 1981) of the *Seattle Times*, who wrote several prize-winning stories on the eruption of volcanic Mount St. Helens in 1980, stressed thinking a story through before the writing begins. ''The mistake that most people make when they are writing on deadline is that they think they can dispense with planning and organizing,'' Zahler said (p. 74). ''I mean taking three or four minutes before you start to think about the material you have, what you have to cover. When I'm writing on deadline, except in the most extreme cases, I take that three of four minutes to make a quick list of the high points of the story and to organize my thinking before I write'' (p. 74). Deadline or not, the advice is still good. With literary feature writing, which usually comes in longer than normal stories, analysis aforethought plays an important role in the writing. Break the story into segments of related information and write a segment at a time.

Likewise, the literary feature writer is careful to write simply. Aristotle warned against writing that is obviously composed and urged that a natural and unstudied manner be used. Nothing fancy, no gimmicks, he said. ''People distrust rhetorical tricks just as they distrust adulterated wines.'' Surmelian (1968, p. 219) advised that good prose has plenty of movement and that the pace is determined by the action in the story: tighter sentences and paragraphs when the action nears climax; more flowing sentences and paragraphs when the action slows. Examples of that approach appear in this book (see, for example, ''It was a day the brave men cried''), and at least one climatic terse ending comes readily to mind, Donald C. Drake's two-word chilling paragraph: ''He fired.''

Literary feature writing must be faithful both to the literary and the journalism. First are the problems of overkill. ''One obvious danger,'' said David Shaw (1981) ''is that some reporters, encouraged to write more colorfully, gratuitously turn a simple story into an orgy of metaphor and simile'' (p. 34). Surmelian (1968) noted that beginning fiction writers have the same problem: ''A common mistake of beginners is to have too many descriptive details in a short story, particularly in the opening paragraphs. They scatter the reader's attention and confuse him, and he loses track of the characters'' (p. 38).

On the journalism side is the question of information. ''If you don't have the horses,'' says Richard Ben Cramer, ''you can't get in the race.'' The other journalists in this book are equally adamant not only about good reporting but also about getting essential details and description so they can write a good story. "I gather all the detail I can," Sager says, "from the size and construction of silos to eye color to the exact number of days it takes corn to grow to maturity, to . . . whatever. . . . I report my stories to death."

In getting detail, Carol McCabe (Clark, 1980) of the *Providence* (Rhode Island) *Journal-Bulletin* does this:

> You ask the questions: What was it like? What did it feel like? Take the reader where he cannot go. You, reporter, go in and bring back information. What is it like in those woods? What is it like on that island? What is it like in that person's dreams? And you do that by accumulating every bit of meaningful detail and using it where it seems appropriate. It's what you leave out sometimes that is as important as what you put in. (p. 116)

Paul Shinoff reveals the kind of questions he asked for his story on the two gravediggers:

> I spent a good part of one day at the cemetery, was there for both the digging and the filling of the grave. I stood next to them, asking questions about the most minute aspects of their work. In such situations, I generally ask a worker to describe what he is doing as he does it. Often, I am asking someone to articulate something that has never been put in words before. And in such situations, the hands move faster than the mouth. "I'm digging," Fitzpatrick would say, feeling a bit silly about the whole thing. I would continue with specific questions. "Why are you holding your hands like that?" "Why that shovel?" We talked a lot about tools.

The point about detail and description in literary feature writing would be belabored were it not central to the fact that literary writing is not possible without relevant detail gleaned through good reporting. Literary feature writers are trying to put the reader in the scene in a variety of ways. Says Gaul: "The only other conscious narrative device I used was emphasis on using clear, well-written visual images." Literary feature writers work exceptionally hard also to convey the character of the people in their stories. Most of them say they achieve that through detail. Beginning journalists, looking for a way to practice gathering and writing detail, might try writing descriptions of photographs. Such an exercise forces the writer not only to look but also to ask questions.

One journalistic element missing or infrequent in literary features is direct quotations. That does not mean no direct quotations at all nor does it mean no quoted dialogue. Frequently, however, it seems that a literarily styled newspaper story can be just as good with a minimum of direct quotations, especially when the story form is reconstruction. In reconstruction, the writer/narrator is telling a story. By not using direct quotations, the writer maintains better control over the story. Direct quotations worth using are those that provide some flavor of the people or move the story along; direct quotations that slowly develop a story can be discarded in favor of the narrator's better phrased pace. What cannot be paraphrased without doing injustice to the tone and flavor of people in the story is telling dialogue, that is, a conversation between two (or more) people. The reporter using dialogue should be present to hear it spoken and not rely on second-hand retrospective sources. When second-hand sources are used, verification is necessary.

It seems almost unnecessary to mention the importance a good lead plays in a literary feature, and the more important point might be the caution against using overstatement, with so much emphasis on style and too little attention to detail, beginning with irrelevant material or at a minor stage in the story. The story cannot start just anywhere. The opening must be relevant to the story's main theme, such as a woman murdering her husband or aliens sneaking across the border in the night. Editors play an important role here, especially when exercising their role as director, as someone to help the writer see the material available and get it moving in the right manner.

The ending of a story is important. A typical newspaper story may just stop, but the literary feature must stop at the right place. How well a story ends is an indication of how well the journalist gathered relevant material and how well the writer controlled the material and understood the process. The best endings stay with the reader long after the reader has turned the page. The best endings endure.

The stories gathered here show that good literary feature writing is possible, that good journalists can write interesting and informative stories in more than one form and still satisfy the highest traditions of journalism. As long as the journalist writing in the literary mode remembers that substance, not style, is the end in journalism, the result should be as journalistically worthy as any other good journalistic effort.

References

Abel, E. (Ed.). (1981). *What's news: The media in American society*. San Francisco: Institute for Contemporary Studies.

Allen, E. S. (July/August 1979). The role of creative writing. *The Bulletin of the American Society of Newspaper Editors*, pp. 3–5.

Barnet, S., Berman, M., & Burto, W. (1971). *A dictionary of literary, dramatic, and cinematic terms* (2nd ed.). Boston: Little, Brown.

Berner, R. T. (1983). The narrative and the headline. *Newspaper Research Journal, 4*(3), 33–39.

Berner, R. T. (1986, October). *Literary newswriting: The death of an oxymoron* (Journalism Monographs No. 99). Columbia, SC: The Association for Education in Journalism and Mass Communication.

Best, E. P. (1981, December). Stockton Record finds 'Roots of Violence'. *The Gannetteer*, pp. 16–17.

Canary, R. H., & Kozicki, H. (Eds.). (1978). *The writing of history: Literary form and historical understanding*. Madison, WI: The University of Wisconsin Press.

Chase, W. M. (1982, January). New journalism isn't new: Fact, fiction and fraud in American newspapers. *The Stanford Observer*, pp. 2–3.

Clark, R. P. (Ed.). (1979). *Best newspaper writing 1979*. St. Petersburg, FL: Modern Media Institute.

Clark, R. P. (Ed.). (1980). *Best newspaper writing 1980*. St. Petersburg, FL: Modern Media Institute.

Clark, R. P. (Ed.). (1981). *Best newspaper writing 1981*. St. Petersburg, FL: Modern Media Institute.

Clark, R. P. (1984, March). A new shape for the news. *Washington Journalism Review*, pp. 46–47.

Cousins, N. (1983). *The healing heart*. New York: W. W. Norton.

Davis, L. J. (1983). *Factual fictions*. New York: Columbia University Press.

Donohew, L. (1982) Newswriting styles: What arouses the reader? *Newspaper Research Journal, 3*(2), 3–6.

Ellis, J. M. (1974). *The theory of literary criticism: A logical analysis*. Berkeley and Los Angeles: University of California Press.

Fontaine, A. (1974). *The art of writing nonfiction*. New York: Thomas Y. Crowell.

Fowler, R. (1977). *Linguistics and the novel*. London and New York: Methuen.

Franklin, J. (1983). 'Literary' journalism brings vitality while providing 'reading pleasure'. *Afternoon Delight* (an Associated Press Managing Editors' report on afternoon newspapers), pp. 17–19.

Franklin, J. (1987). Myths of literary journalism: a practitioner's perspective. *Journalism Educator, 42*(3) pp. 8–13.

Gaul, G. M. (1986, July 13). The deluge at the Big Lick Mountain mine. *Inquirer Magazine*, pp. 11–13, 35.

Gibson, W. (1966). *Tough, sweet & stuffy. An essay on modern American prose styles.* Bloomington, IN: Indiana University Press.

Hellmann, J. (1981). *Fables of fact: The new journalism as new fiction.* Urbana, Chicago, London: University of Illinois Press.

Hersey, J. (1949, November). The novel of contemporary history. *Atlantic Monthly,* pp. 80, 82, 84.

Lopez, B. (1984, December). Story at Anaktuvuk Pass: At the junction of landscape and narrative. *Harper's,* pp. 49–52.

Lyons, L. M. (Ed.). (1965). *Reporting the news: Selections from Nieman Reports.* Cambridge, MA: The Belknap Press of Harvard University.

Malcolm, A. H. (1986, February 14). Fateful choice in fatal illness: How long to live. *New York Times,* p. A12.

Murphy, J. E. (1974, May). *The new journalism: A critical perspective.* (Journalism Monographs No. 34). Lexington, KY: The Association for Education in Journalism.

National News Council. (1981). *After 'Jimmy's World': Tightening up in editing. A report by the National News Council.* New York: Author.

Rodgers, G. (1983). Reading needn't be a chore. *Afternoon Delight* (an Associated Press Managing Editors' report on afternoon newspapers), p. 17.

Sager, M. (1981, December 6). The hunt: Special bond for father, son. *The Washington Post,* pp. 1, 25.

Schudson, M. (1978). *Discovering the news.* New York: Basic Books.

Snyder, L. L., & Morris, R. B. (Eds.). (1962). *A treasury of great reporting* (2nd ed.). New York: Simon & Schuster.

Surmelian, L. (1968). *Techniques of fiction writing: Measure and madness.* Garden City, NY: Doubleday Anchor.

Tannebaum, P. H. (1953). The effect of headlines on the interpretation of news stories. *Journalism Quarterly,* pp. 189–97.

Weber, R. (1980). *The literature of fact.* Athens, OH: Ohio University Press.

Yagoda, B. (1986, August 10). No tense like the present. *The New York Times Book Review,* pp. 1, 30.

Author Index

Subject Index